The Dynamic,

Fundamental Study On Discipleship
Enter If You Are Teachable!

Dr. James Whorley

author HOUSE

AuthorHouse™
1663 Liberty Drive
Bloomington, IN 47403
www.authorhouse.com
Phone: 833-262-8899

Published by AuthorHouse 03/07/2023

ISBN: 979-8-8230-0152-6 (sc)
ISBN: 979-8-8230-0233-2 (e)

Library of Congress Control Number: 2023903761

Print information available on the last page.

Any people depicted in stock imagery provided by Getty Images are models,
and such images are being used for illustrative purposes only.
Certain stock imagery © Getty Images.

This book is printed on acid-free paper.

Because of the dynamic nature of the Internet, any web addresses or links contained in this book may have changed
since publication and may no longer be valid. The views expressed in this work are solely those of the author and do
not necessarily reflect the views of the publisher, and the publisher hereby disclaims any responsibility for them.

CONTENTS

INTRODUCTION

This is a book written out of my concern of seeing so many people getting saved, as they might say. You see this in large rallies, church conventions, stadiums, etc. They are emotionally touched and moved to act, but later, they fall off, because they were not taught how to walk with Jesus and how to live out their Christian life.

This book has been written to teach them the importance of their salvation, the purpose of their calling and how to maintain a spirit-filled life.

It will be very important that one has a teachable spirit, able to be taught, maintain a consistency and drive throughout the book.

There is no doubt in my mind that you will learn things that you may not have ever considered, but dig in, strap down and get ready for a wonderful journey and experience!

CHAPTER 1

Knowing and Understanding Your Calling

Introduction

This will be a thirteen-chapter study of discipleship. Discipleship teaches that you are a student and apprentice striving to ascertain the knowledge of the teaching.

In our thirteen-chapter study, we will be studying the grass roots of the life of Jesus Christ and his teachings and life lessons to the disciples.. We will be focusing on the calling, the fellowship, faith, kingdom, death, burial, resurrection, and the instructions he left them to proceed.

We would like you to note the different backgrounds and lifestyles of the disciples. You will be able to evaluate your own beginning and clearly identify your own spiritual growth.

Our main objective through these lessons will be to give one a clear step-by-step path through the life of a true disciple.

We would ask that as you start these chapters, you faithfully commit to becoming a person of understanding and knowledge who has the wisdom to easily perform these lessons in a daily application.

SESSION 1

THE CALLING/COMMANDS THAT WERE GIVEN TO FOLLOW

Calling—"A strong urge toward a particular way of life or career; a vocation".

Follow"—Go or come after (a person or thing proceeding ahead); move or travel behind. Come after in time or order; act according to (an instruction or precept); strive after; aim at".

Matthew 28:19–20 is an explanation of our calling to go forward making disciples. We have been sent forth by our master and king, Jesus Christ, who has given us his authority and power to fully recognize that it's not going to be achieved by our power but the power that has been given to us by Christ Jesus. It also gives the central purpose for all believers.

Our lives belong not to us but to the one who died to purchase our freedom from sin and death. We disregard the significance of his command when we fail to fulfill the great commission that he has placed upon our lives. In other words, we as disciples are no longer our own but are bought with a price.

We will become true disciples of the Messiah, effectively reproducing other disciples, if we abide with him and live out what we learn from him. Our focus is to make disciples.

What's important in our mission is to reproduce in others what Jesus has produced in us (love, authority, compassion, growth, faith, boldness, and a powerful, true message as his witnesses). We are disciples commanded to produce more disciples.

By fulfilling the teaching portion of the great commission, we must take believers at all stages of spiritual maturity to the next stage of growth. This can range from the infancy of a brand-new believer to many other levels of spiritual adulthood. Also, we must keep in mind what Romans 11:29 states: "For the gifts and calling of God are without repentance." As you can see, the calling has been on one's life before one repented.

It is important to note that one's character (the behavior of an individual) should begin to take on the form of the word of God, constantly growing, developing, and maturing.

A. As being a spiritual leader, I would advise one to do as Luke 14:28 states: "For which of you, intending to build a tower, sitteth not down first, and counteth the cost whether he have sufficient to finish it?" It is important for one to be prudent (before proceeding into a matter, carefully look into the situation to complete the objective).

B. When becoming a disciple, one must understand that we are servants of God. We no longer have our own purpose, because we are bought with a price and are no longer the servants of humankind but servants of God, according to 1 Corinthians 7:22–24 (please read).

C. Here, we will clearly see our calling. First Corinthians 1:26 says, "For ye see your calling, brethren, how that not many wise men after the flesh, not many mighty, not many noble are called."

The Lord wants us to realize that without completely depending on him, we can't be effective in bringing disciples to the Lord. As in Moses's time, the people had to completely depend on God for water in the desert and for bread from on high.

We will understand our effectiveness if we would realize, according to 1 Corinthians 1:29, "That no flesh should glory in his presence."

D. We must remember that in fulfilling our calling, we must be passionate in our desire to please the one who called us.

The scripture has declared that the harvest is plenteous and ready for harvesting. "Pray ye therefore the Lord of the harvest, that he will send forth laborers into his harvest." Luke 10:2. My friends, the true reality of this scripture is that we are actually praying for ourselves, for we are the laborers who are needed to become harvesters.

You should easily answer these four questions after studying this lesson.

Questions:

1. What is the meaning of *calling*?

2. What is the meaning of *discipleship*?

3. What does the first chapter of 1 Corinthians define as our calling?

4. What does the lesson tell us about counting up the cost before one starts the journey of being a disciple?

SESSION 2

WHO PARTICULARLY IS THE LORD CALLING TO BE DISCIPLES?

These are the names of the twelve disciples the Lord called: Peter, Andrew, James, John, Philip, Bartholomew, Thomas, Matthew, James, Thaddaeus, Simon, and Judas.

As we can see, these men came from different walks of life. There was a doctor, tax collectors, fishermen, publicans, and of course, sinners. This makes one think of people who have been called into the military. They come from all parts of the country and include hippies, bikers, and farmers. When coming to boot camp, they have all come for one main purpose: to be molded and established as soldiers. If one were to ask them what their specific reasons were for becoming, a soldier, they would give you different answers, such as, "My life wasn't going anywhere," "My life seems not to have any direction," "I wanted to be a part of something that is meaningful," or "I was told that this would be the best way for a young person to start his or her life."

On day one, they meet their drill sergeant. His objective is to tear down their sense of support that they may have had when they arrived. Their new support and strength will come from their willingness to learn and adapt to the orders and instructions that will be given by their drill sergeants. What they will learn is that old things have passed away, and they must obtain this new way of living. The old must be released and the new must be ascertained.

New soldiers going through these life-skill trainings will learn determination, focus, teamwork, discipline, temperance, and the importance of following and obeying instructions. This is why we are comparing a soldier with discipleship. One will need such focus and discipline in his or her pursuit of becoming well rounded.

Our Lord Jesus, in the calling of his disciples, is requiring that they deny (refuse to accept, recognize, or believe) themselves.

> "Then said Jesus unto his disciples, if any man will come after me, let him deny himself, and take up his cross, and follow me. For whosoever will save his life shall lose it: and whosoever will lose his life for my sake shall find it. For what is a man profited, if he shall gain the whole world, and lose his own soul? Or what shall a man give in exchange for

his soul? For the son of man shall come in the glory of his Father with his angels; and then he shall reward every man according to his works. (Matthew 16:24–27)"

Many may think that they can follow Christ on their own terms, but this is truly far from the actual truth. We, as disciples, have no concept of how one can fulfill the purpose of Christ. Therefore, we must submit totally to the master's instructions. In this submission, to deny oneself with this depth of denial is to live without a single thread of self-centered thought, devoted exclusively to Jesus and his work. One must also be able to identify with Christ by taking up his or her own personal cross, meaning one's willingness to die from one's own will, taking on wholeheartedly the will of Christ.

I would like to show you why I believe that many Christians become disorientated in their pursuit to save their lives. They become so caught up in receiving praise and accolades from humankind that they lose what is truly important.

We have been called by Christ to become disciples. Therefore, our main objective is to please him only, giving all glory to Christ in the way we live and pursue eternal life.

When we are reaching for souls, preaching in our pulpits, singing in our choirs, or ushering in our churches, we should strive to lose who we are and take on fully the identity of Christ in our actions, knowing that we are living epistles, known and read by all whom we meet. In these scriptures, Christ is striving to get us to see the true importance of saving our lives and not losing it.

In our lesson, we are asked to note Matthew 16:26- "For what is a man profited, if he shall gain the whole world, and lose his soul?" According to Ecclesiastes the second chapter, all that man gain is vanity (the quality of being worthless or futile). In other words, we are saying, Why consume a host of things that are meaningless, or not focus on that which is essential (one's soul), and stand before the final judge and be lost?

The Lord's intent is to motivate the disciples to work wholeheartedly so that they may receive their just rewards.

Colossian 3:23 states, "And whatsoever ye do, do it heartily, as to the Lord, and not unto men." Therefore, as we stated previously, if a soldier stays committed, he or she will be transformed into a full-pledged soldier. The soldier's language, walk, manner, conversation, actions, and all that "was" when he or she started will now be a complete metamorphosis of whom the soldier has become. Similarly, a disciple in name will become a disciple indeed.

Romans 12:1-2 states – "I beseech you, brethren, by the mercies of God, that ye present your bodies a living sacrifice, holy acceptable unto God, which is your reasonable service. (2) and be not conformed to this world: but be ye transformed by the renewing of your mind, that ye may prove what is that good, and acceptable, and perfect will of God."

QUESTIONS:

1. Who did God call particularly to be a disciple?

2. Why do you think a comparison was made between a disciple and soldier?

3. What does it mean to deny oneself?

4. How can I present myself as a living sacrifice?

SESSION 3

THE LIGHT

John 8:12- "Then spake Jesus again unto them, saying, I am the light of the world: he that followeth me shall not walk in darkness, but shall have the light of life."

Here the Lord is establishing that he is undoubtedly, unquestionably the light. The opposite of light (shines, directs, make clear, points out) is darkness, which is sin, one separated from God, disobedient and lost.

As being disciples, there are so many different philosophies, teachings and ethnics. All striving for followers, but one must understand that Jesus, according to John 14:6 "is the way, the truth and life." A disciple must be strong and bold in his belief, that in Jesus was life and in him was the light of men according to John 1:4. As disciples, we are unique and separated totally from the world.

The bible declares that the world love darkness and hate the light. Our love for Jesus has caused us to be unique and particular as salt and light according to Matthew 5:13-16. In these verses, we will clearly understand that we have been called to be salt and also called to be light. Matthew 5:13- "Ye are the salt of the earth: but if the salt have lost his savour, wherewith shall it be salted? It is thenceforth good for nothing, but to be cast out, and to be trodden under foot of men. (14) Ye are the light of the world. A city that is set on an hill cannot be hid.

(15) Neither do men light a candle, and put it under a bushel, but on a candlestick; and it giveth light unto all that are in the house. (16) Let your light so shine before men, that they may see your good works, and glorify your father which is in heaven."

As we consider the meaning of salt, which is used for seasoning and to preserve food, the bible explains discipleship as an example of salt, demonstrating that we are the seasoning to give the world that which they need and may not realize it. We are also the preservatives to give the world the substance which they need to live.

I've eaten many meals with all types of herbs, but without salt, the meal is evidently incomplete, just as man is incomplete without his submission and surrendering to the Savior.

I hope that our mandate is clearly obvious that we have been called as leaders in a world that needs direction. We must therefore be effective in being salt that has not lost its savouring. Salt that has lost its savouring will be overlooked, no good and trampled under the feet of men.

Hear now, the disciples of the most high! Thou calling again is most clear. The Lord has declared that ye are the light. The world is truly in darkness and your calling is to lead them out of darkness, unto Christ.

As the scriptures has established us as being men and women living after the ordinance of Christ, walking daily in the fruit of the spirit, denying the foolishness of the lust of this world, we must have this purpose in mind, that the world truly needs us to walk whole-heartedly in our calling.

Let's take note of the 58th chapter of the book of Isaiah. It explains to us that when true disciples are serious about their purpose, these are some of the things that shall occur: loosed bands of wickedness, undoing of heavy burdens, the oppressed set free and every yoke broken, your light break forth as the morning, your health spring forth speedily, your righteousness go before you and the Lord shall be your rereward.

I Peter 2:9 – "But ye are a chosen generation, a royal priesthood, an holy nation, a peculiar people; that ye should shew forth the praises of him who hath called you out of darkness into his marvelous light."

The Lord wants us all to know that we are special and greatly loved as he has called us in this generation to reach a people that he desires that they should not perish, but repent and come unto him.

QUESTIONS:

1. Who is the light and what does it mean to be a light?

2. What is salt? What and who is depict to be salt and in what capacity?

3. How did we become the light and in what capacity?

4. What are some things that we can do to harm our discipleship as being a Light?

CHAPTER 2

Follow Me and I Will Make You

SESSION 1

PRESENT YOUR BODY

Make- "Create or produce something by working; form something by breaking, cutting etc. Form by putting parts together or combining substances; construct, create. To cause to exist or come about."

As we can see, the making of one is the total reconstruction of what one was and the total reconstruction of what the maker wants one to become.

It must be established in one's mind that Jesus is our creator. This is why it is essential for us to according to Romans 12: 2-3 "present our bodies a living sacrifice, holy and acceptable unto God, which is our reasonable service. Conforming not unto this world, but being transformed by the renewing of our mind, proving what is that good, acceptable and perfect will of God. Also, understanding that to every man that is among you, not to think of himself more highly than he ought to think: but to think soberly, according as God hath delt to every man the measure of faith."

Now, let us strive to break these scriptures down into smaller bites so that they would be easier to digest: Present your body- meaning to give of yourself as a living sacrifice, willing to fulfill the process (a series of actions or steps taken to achieve a particular end). This is where His will becomes our will and our cross becomes clearly apparent.

We accept the breaking, tearing down, submitting, getting rid of our goals or plans and submitting to the reason that we have been called. Our maker will make us holy and acceptable unto God, which is impossible for us to do, except we go through the process.

Please understand that in the process of being made, nothing of the world must be implemented. Our desires must be focused on becoming like our maker. Therefore, even the totality of our thoughts must be united with our maker as we are transformed as true disciples.

As in often times, as one looking into great tasks, we feel a need to implement our own actions in getting things done, but the Lord wants us to know that it is by his grace and not for us to think of ourselves greater than we are. In other words, stay out of the way and leave it to the maker. This is the very reason that he has given us the measure of faith, that we as disciples would utilize our faith and keep our flesh under subjection.

Ephesians 4:11-13 "And he gave some, apostles; and some, prophets; and some, evangelists; and some, pastors and teachers; For the perfecting of the saints, for the work of the ministry, for the edifying of the body of Christ: Till we all come in the unity of the faith, and of the knowledge of the Son of God, unto a perfect man unto the measure of the stature of the fulness of Christ:"

This is why it is essential for us that are disciples to be willing to submit to our instructor, believing that their (the Instructors) purpose is to bring us into perfection.

The word of God tells us in Hebrews 13:7- "Remember them which have the rule over you, who have spoken unto you the word of God: whose faith follow, considering the end of their conversation." Re-emphasizing this important command by stating it again in this same chapter, in the 17th verse "Obey them that have the rule over you, and submit yourselves: for they watch for your souls, as they that must give account, that they may do it with joy, and not with grief: for that is unprofitable for you." This is why it is so important for us to be humble enough to become teachable hearers and doers of the spoken word.

QUESTIONS

1. Who is the Maker and what is being made?

2. If I want to be made, what is my first plan of action?

3. Why is it essential that I submit to another authority, when I have my own opinions?

4. What is the purpose of those that are called in the fivefold ministry?

SESSION 2

<u>LOVE ME WITH ALL YOUR HEART</u>

The Lord understands the total love commitment necessary for one to have to be willing to endure this necessary process to be a disciple of Christ. Luke 14:26- "If any man come to me, and hate not his father, and mother, and wife, and children, and brethren, and sisters, yea, and his own life also, he can not be my disciple."

I would like for you to understand that the Lord is not asking you to hate those that are close to you, but when it comes to the Lord, your love commitment, diligence and relationship should supersede all. If you truly and not just talking desire to be a true disciple, this is what it will take.

If any of those that are close to you come in between your personal relationship with Christ, don't allow yourself to be perverted (having been corrupted or distorted from its original course, meaning or state) from your love and commitment to Christ.

Examples:

(A)   If your mate strives to pervert your commitment, stand firm!

(B)   If your children or relatives strives to pervert your diligence, stand firm!

(C)   If your job or fleshly desires strives to make the things of God insignificant, stand firm!

(D)   If a preacher or angel seemeth to have come from on high, come perverting the true word of God, stand firm!

In the Book of Genesis, the scripture describes certain tests that Abraham went through to prove his word and diligence to the word of God. His faith was being developed as the maker walked him through these events.

1.   Abraham was commanded to leave his family to search for a city that the Lord would show him and he obeyed.

2.   Abraham loved Hagar and her son Ishmael, but was commanded to give them up. He obeyed and complied.

3. Abraham loved Isaac. The son that came through the promise. He was commanded to offer up Isaac as a sacrifice. He complied, obeyed and by faith, was introduced to one of the greatest names of Christ. Jehovah Jireh (God will provide).

Luke 14:27-"And whosoever doth not bear his cross, and come after me, can not be my disciple."

One may ask themself, what is my cross? The answer is, the works of the flesh. Galatians 5:19-"Now the works of the flesh are manifest, which are these; Adultery (any type of sexual behavior outside of marriage), fornication (any type of sexual behavior before marriage), uncleanness (foulness, dirtiness, filthiness), lasciviousness (excite lust, and promote irregular indulgences), idolatry (the worship of idols, images or anything made by hands, or which is not God), witchcraft (the spirit of stubbornness, disobedience, spiritual enchantments and wicked powers), hatred (great dislike), variance (differences that produces dispute or controversy, disagreement or discord), emulations (striving to out-do others to receive the recognition or praise of man), wrath (violent anger), strife (contention in anger, quarreling), sedition (conduct or speech causing people to rebel against authority), heresies (standing against and speaking against sound doctrine), envyings (covetousness with regard to another's advantages, possessions, or attainments), murders (physical or verbal premeditated killing of one human-being by another), drunkenness (controlled by demonic spirits), revellings (being excited about your enemy's misfortune), and such like: of the which I tell you before, as I have also told you in time past, that they which do such things shall not inherit the kingdom of God."

QUESTIONS FROM SESSION 2

1. What type of love commitment do God require?

2. Why do you think that such a love commitment is required for change?

3. In our lesson, what is depict as the cross?

4. What will happen to those that live according to the works of the flesh?

SESSION 3

<u>THE WORD PLANTED IN GOOD GROUND</u>

John 8:31-32 "Then said Jesus to those Jews which believed on him, If you continue in my word, then are ye my disciples indeed; And ye shall know the truth, and the truth shall make you free."

The scripture here is showing you that the word of God is alive. If one continue in it (reading, meditating and pondering upon it), it will cause definite transformation. This is why we see so great of emphasis on studying God's word for a total life change. I guarantee you that if one becomes steadfast in God's word, he will grow and develope into a powerful love, faith and bold disciple of Jesus Christ.

You need to know and understand that the word of God is a seed and our heart is the ground that the seed is planted in.

Matthew 13:3-4 "And he spake many things unto them in parables, saying, behold, a sower went forth to sow; And when he sowed, some seeds fell by the way side, and the fowls came and devoured them up:" This means - Matthew 13:19- "When any one heareth the word of the kingdom, and understandeth it not, then cometh the wicked one, and catcheth away that which was sown in his heart. This is he which received seed by the way side." An individual's lack of consistency causes the word of God to be easily removed. Having nothing within them to hold them, they easily give up and fall away.

Matthew 13:5-6- "Some fell upon stony places, where they had not much earth: and forthwith they sprung up, because they had no deepness of earth: And when the sun was up, they were scorched; and because they had no root, they withered away." This means- Matthew 13:20-21- "But he that received the seed into stony places, the same is he that heareth the word, and anon with joy receiveth it; Yet hath he not root in himself, but dureth for a while: for when tribulation or persecution ariseth because of the word, by and by he is offended." This is what happens to people who are caught up into feelings. Joyous one day and then the reality of what it takes to be in the relationship with Christ is revealed unto them, they're not willing to endure. They then give up.

Matthew 13:7- "And some fell among thorns; and the thorns sprung up, and choked them:" This meaning- Matthew 13:22- "He also that received seed among thorns is he that heareth the word; and the care of this world, and the deceitfulness of riches, choke the word, and he becometh unfruitful." Sad to say, that these are the people who have been in the church for years, full of worldly cares, not growing, not seeing the hand of God and are dead while they are confessing that they are alive.

Matthew 13:23- "But he that received seed into the good ground is he that heareth the word, and understandeth it; which also beareth fruit, and bringeth forth, some a hundredfold, some sixty, some thirty." Here, we see that the word is truly alive. When the word says that you are blessed, you are blessed. When the word says that you shall prosper and be in health as your soul prosper, you shall obtain it.

Disciples of God, you will truly obtain, achieve and become all that the word of God declares!

QUESTIONS -SESSION 3

1. In our lesson, what is the word of God depict as?

2. In our lesson, what is the ground depict as?

3. In our lesson, The void of something causes an individual to fall every time. What is that?

4. Explain: What should one receive if the word falls upon good ground?

EVANGELIZING
THE GROWTH OF A CHURCH

A. **ME**-SIX MONTHS REACHES **PATTY**. SIX MONTHS LATER, **PATTY** REACHES **JIM**. **ME**-REACHES **MIKE**, FIRST YEAR- **FOUR SOULS** ARE ADDED TO THE CHURCH.

B. SIX MONTHS LATER, WORKING DILIGENTLY OUR **FOUR SOULS** REACHES AN **ADDITIONAL FOUR SOULS**. SIX MONTHS LATER THE SECOND YEAR, **OUR EIGHT HAS DOUBLED TO SIXTEEN**. THEREFORE. THE CHURCH HAS GROWN TO THE TOTAL OF **SIXTEEN**.

C. **THE SIXTEEN**, SIX MONTHS LATER, BEING FAITHFUL AND WORKING DILIGENTLY, HAS DOUBLED THEMSELVES TO THE TOTAL OF **THIRTY-TWO**. AFTER SIX ADDITIONAL MONTHS HAS GROWN TO **SIXTY-FOUR**. STARTING WITH ONLY **ME**, THE CHURCH **IN THREE YEARS**, HAS **GROWN TO ONE-HUNDRED AND TWENTY-EIGHT DISCIPLES**.

IMAGINE **IF WE HAD FIVE ME'S**, WORKING ON THIS DUPLICATING PROCESS, WE **WOULD HAVE HAD FIVE TIMES ONE-HUNDRED AND TWENTY-EIGHT AFTER THREE YEARS**, WHICH **WOULD HAVE BEEN A TOTAL OF SIX-HUNDRED AND FORTY**.

OF COURSE, WE MUST ALLOW FOR HUMAN ERROR AND THE LACK OF ONE BEING PERSISTENT, BUT EVEN IF HALF OF THE DISCIPLES ARE FAITHFUL, THREE-HUNDRED AND TWENTY NEW DISCIPLES WOULD BE A BLESSING TO ANY CHURCH.

CHAPTER 3

THE KINGDOM OF GOD
RIGHTEOUSNESS/ETHICALLY RIGHT

THE KINGDOM OF SATAN
DEVILISH, EVIL, SELFISH, PRIDE

SESSION 1

THE KINGDOM OF GOD

TOPIC: OUR DISTINCTNESS

Distinctness- "The quality or state of being different; Being different from that otherwise experienced or known."

Kingdom- "The spiritual sovereignty of God or Christ. The dominion over which the spiritual sovereignty of God or Christ extends, whether in heaven or on the earth."

As we begin to learn about the kingdom of God, we must embrace God's distinctness (God is the kingdom different from all other kingdoms, because his kingdom is sovereign). There is none that can duplicate such great majesty and awesomeness of this great kingdom.

God is the sole Creator of all that exist. As one observes the uniqueness of every living organism in the plant world, cold and warm-blooded living creatures, one can't help but to be in total awe. Our great God created man-kind to serve, honor and glorify him and him alone.

Man was given by God, dominion over the entire earth and was commanded to subdue (bring under control) it and also to increase and replenish the earth. We clearly see God's love in that which he created and his desire to have personal fellowship with man-kind.

Man broke the distinct fellowship with his creator by listening and obeying Satan, causing death and evil to enter into the world. Therefore, we can clearly see the kingdom of God and how Satan sieged the kingdom of man and how man began to obey the words of Satan.

We see clearly, the utter destruction of the influence of the kingdom of Satan and its affect on man-kind. The actions of man-kind caused him to be cast from the garden, losing his access to the tree of life which gave him eternal life.

The Lord began a process of striving to get the kingdom of God back into the hearts of man, in which it would give him the power to reign.

When the Lord, in chapter six of Genesis declared that "it repented him that he had made man on the earth, and it grieved him at his heart, because that every imagination of the thoughts of man's heart was only evil continually," He said that "the end of all flesh had come before him and that he will destroy them with the earth."

The Lord in his distinctness and infinite wisdom, chose a man by the name of Abram, whereby he began to establish a people that would walk by faith and not by sight. The Lord would carry this out by giving him a son from his wife Sarai who was barren. This promised son would have two sons of his own by the names of Esau and Jacob.

The Lord blessed Jacob to have twelve sons and through these sons, the twelve tribes of Israel would be established. Here, you will see the splendidness and awesomeness of God's plan unfolding as the kingdom that was once stolen reestablished.

God multiplied his nation as one would place eggs into an incubator until they were hatched and ready to go forth. God will show his sovereign power as he rips his nation from a nation with the might of his powerful hand. They would come forth as an exodus leaving their slave masters, freeing them to go forth, enabling them to praise God and pursue the land that the Almighty had promised! Exodus 19:6- "And ye shall be unto me a kingdom of priests, and an holy nation."

Our Heavenly Father desires to fellowship with his great nation, therefore he gave them commandments and laws to abide by and to establish their moral character.

A. The Lord fulfilled his promise of giving the children of Israel the promised land through Joshua, conquering the nation of the Canaanites. Joshua declaring that "all the Lord has promised you, has been fulfilled in your ears this day."

B. The next dispensation (particular events or occurrences that take place at a certain period of time), took the kingdom to a time where they were under judges to instruct and lead them in the ways of God.

C. The Lord gave unto Israel, prophets that would hear the voice of God, which in turn would deliver his word unto the people. After Samuel, the people requested and desired a king.

D. In the dispensation during the reign of kings, major and minor prophets, the people fell under the hands of man. Four hundred years would pass until the coming of Jesus Christ (the Kingdom manifested in the flesh).

QUESTION CHAPTER 3 - SESSION 1

1. In our lesson, you were given the meaning of kingdom. Can you give me that meaning?

2. In our lesson, you were shown the importance of being distinct. Can you explain that meaning?

3. Whose kingdom did Satan take power over?

4. As studying man's walk with God, something seems to keep re-occurring. Explain

SESSION 2

THY KINGDOM COME

In our previous lesson, we were taught how that the Creator established the Kingdom upon the earth and how that kingdom was stolen and re-created by God's divine plan.

In this present lesson, we will show you directly God's Kingdom and how it was manifested in man-kind's life.

A. Hebrews 12:28- "Wherefore we receiving a kingdom which cannot be moved, let us have grace, whereby we may serve God acceptably with reverence and godly fear:"

We see here, the Kingdom of God is unmovable, sovereign (supreme ruler), omnipotent (unlimited power; able to do anything), omniscience (knowing everything) and omnipresent (being present anywhere or everywhere at the same time), therefore, we as God's servants, should reverence him and whole-heartedly be committed to obeying and following all of his commandments.

B. Hebrews 1:8- "But unto the Son he saith, Thy throne, O God, is for ever and ever: a Sceptre (imperial authority; sovereignty) of righteousness is the Sceptre of thy kingdom."

Our lesson shows clearly being the righteousness (the quality of being morally right or justifiable), as one committed to following the precious word of God.

In the sixth chapter of the book of Matthew, we are commanded not to worry about the matters of this life, but to "seek ye first the Kingdom of God and his righteousness and all these things will be added unto us". We are commanded once again, that "the Kingdom of God is not meat and drink; but righteousness, and peace and joy in the Holy Ghost." (Romans 14:17).

C. "John declared that he was not that light, but he was sent to bear witness of that light" (John 1:8), therefore, he proclaimed that "the kingdom of God is at hand" (Matthew 3:2). John also proclaimed – "And I knew him not: but he that sent me to baptize with water, the same said unto me, Upon whom thou shalt see the Spirit descending, and remaining on him, the same is he which baptizeth with the Holy Ghost. And I saw, and bare record that this is the Son of God" (John 1:33-34).

D.   Our Lord and Savior, Jesus Christ came proclaiming a similar message. (John 3rd chapt., 14th verse) "Jesus answered and said unto him, Verily, verily, I say unto thee, Except a man be born again, he cannot see the Kingdom of God."

Throughout the Old Testament, we see the constant failure of mankind, because of the weakness of his flesh. The Lord understood that if man would have any chance of making it back unto him (the Lord), he would have to dwell within man-kind, reconciling man back unto himself.

The Lord recognized that man willingly walked away from his Creator, causing death and separation from eternal life. The Lord therefore, would have to destroy the power of the flesh by overcoming and triumphing over it. Our Lord and Savior accomplished this by defeating the power of death and the grave (I Corinthians 15:54-57). "So when this corruptible shall have put on incorruption and this mortal shall have put on immortality, then shall be brought to pass the saying that is written, Death is swallowed up in victory. O death, where is thy sting? O grave, where is thy victory? The sting of death is sin; and the strength of sin is the law. But thanks be to God, which giveth us the victory through our Lord Jesus Christ."

As we can see, that which man lost in the garden, life and eternal life through death, The Lord has now given us victory that we have life and have it more abundantly. These are a few things that we have received in the results of our new birth:

1.   Romans 6:3-4 – "know ye not, that so many of us as were baptized into Jesus Christ were baptized into his death? Therefore we are buried with him by baptism into death: that like as Christ was raised up from the dead by the glory of the Father, even so we also should walk in newness of life."

Whereby one is able to see that we are well on our way, as father Abraham, looking for that city whose builder and maker is God.

2.   Ephesians 1:3 – "Blessed be the God and Father of our Lord Jesus Christ, who hath blessed us with all spiritual blessings in heavenly places in Christ:"

The Lord has fully equipped us with all that's necessary to occupy and have full dominion in this present world.

3.   II Corinthians 10:4-5- "For the weapons of our warfare are not carnal, but mighty through God to the pulling down of strong holds: Casting down

imaginations, and every high thing that exalteth itself against the knowledge of God, and bringing into captivity every thought to the obedience of Christ;"

The Lord has truly given us mighty weapons to use and to function in, as we boldly walk in the Kingdom of God.

4. For one to be effective in the Kingdom of God, we must learn to walk in the spirit and not in the flesh. According to I Thessalonians 5:23, which tells us that we are a spirit, we have a soul and that we live in a body. It is essential that if we are to live in God's spiritual kingdom, we must walk in the spirit.

I can't emphasize enough, that we must learn that we are a spirit, we must allow the spirit of God to lead us and we must meditate on following after the spiritual things God.

The word of God declares that "the Lord searches for such (true worshippers) to worship him in spirit and in truth" (John 4:24). Many make mistakes of thinking that we are a body and live after the things of the flesh and the results of this, will cause us never to be able to walk in the supernatural things of Jesus Christ.

I Thessalonians 4:17 – "Then we which are alive and remain shall be caught up together with them in the clouds, to meet the Lord in the air: and so shall we ever be with the Lord."

I John 3:3- "And every man that hath this hope in him purifieth himself, even as he is pure."

QUESTIONS CHAPTER 3 SESESSION 2

1. What is the meaning of distinct?

2. After the death of Joshua, what dispensation occurred?

3. For the kingdom of God is not meat and drink; Please complete this verse.

4. What would you consider the difference between the Old Testament and the New Testament?

SESSION 3

THE KINGDOM OF DARKNESS

I take no pleasure in writing nor discussing Satan's kingdom, but it is quite necessary for the disciples to be able to clearly identify when Satan is at work.

The scripture tells us that Satan comes with all deceivableness (deceived or misled) and lying wonders. II Thessalonians 2:9-10 – "Even him, whose coming is after the working of Satan with all power and signs and lying wonders, And with all deceivableness of unrighteousness in them that perish; because they received not the love of the truth, that they might be saved."

We would like for you to clearly see that Satan has not the power as one might think, but he strives to work against the body and the mind. There is another tool commonly used by Satan which is that of lying. John 8:44 – "Ye are of your father the devil, and the lusts of your father ye will do. He was a murderer from the beginning, and abode not in the truth, because there is no truth in him. When he speaketh a lie, he speaketh of his own: for he is a liar, and the father of it."

Below are a few examples of Satan's lying and deceptive actions toward God's people:

1. Satan deceived a portion of heaven. Jude 1:6- "And the angels which kept not their first estate, but left their own habitation, he hath reserved in everlasting chains unto the judgement of the great day".

2. Satan deceived Adam and Eve, causing the fall of all mankind. Genesis 3:6 –7 "And when the woman saw that the tree was good for food, and that it was pleasant to the eyes, and a tree to be desired to make one wise, she took of the fruit thereof, and did eat, and gave also unto her husband with her; and he did eat. And the eyes of them both were opened, and they knew that they were naked; and they sewed fig leaves together, and made themselves aprons."

3. Satan deceived man-kind once again, causing God to destroy the world with water. Genesis 6:7- "And the Lord said, I will destroy man whom I have created from the face of the earth; both man and beast, and the creeping thing, and the fowls of the air; for it repenteth me that I have made them."

4. Satan lied and deceived Judas Iscariot to betray the Lord. Matthew 10:4 – Simon the Canaanite, and Judas Iscariot who also betrayed him."

Please note how often Satan used deception as a weapon. The scriptures let us know that "if it was possible, Satan would deceive the very elect." This is why it is essential for us to know (intimately) the truth, that regardless of what we are told or what we see, we will not allow it to deceive us.

Satan's ultimate plan is to destroy the Kingdom of God and all who follow God. The liar (Satan) believes that he will sit upon the throne of God and eventually rule all that the Creator made. Isaiah 14:12-14- "How art thou fallen from heaven, O Lucifer, son of the morning! How art thou cut down to the ground, which didst weaken the nations! For thou hast said in thine heart, I will ascend into heaven, I will exalt my throne above the stars of God: I will sit also upon the mount of the congregation, in the sides of the north: I will ascend above the heights of the clouds; I will be like the most High."

I would like to show you that the lack of holding to the truth allows an entrance way for Satan to come in. Acts 5:3 shows that the love of money caused Ananias to lie to the Holy Ghost. His life and his wife's life was taken. Acts 26:18 – Shows us that Satan has a power to keep one in darkness by blinding their eyes, but the gospel preached will deliver them to the light of righteousness.

Satan has the power to war against our flesh, destroying our flesh if we refuse to obey and follow the truth. I Corinthians 5:5- "To deliver such an one unto Satan for the destruction of the flesh, that the spirit may be saved in the day of the Lord Jesus."

The bible warns us to forgive and not hold anything in our hearts, because if we do, we are giving Satan an advantage. In other words, we give him an inroad into our lives. II Corinthians 2:11- "Lest Satan should get an advantage of us: for we are not ignorant of his devices."

Remember, Satan can use ministers, singers or even himself to be transformed into an angel of light, to deceive with part lies and part truth. II Corinthians 11:13-15-"For such are false apostles, deceitful workers, transforming themselves into the apostles of Christ. And no marvel; for Satan himself is transformed into an angel of light. Therefore it is no great thing if his ministers also be transformed as the minister of righteousness; whose end shall be according to their works."

Satan come to steal, kill and destroy, finding entry ways into our lives through the gateways of our senses. Our eye gate, ear gate, mouth gate, nose gate and touch gate.

Galatians 6:7-9 – "Be not deceived; God is not mocked: for whatsoever a man soweth, that shall he also reap. For he that soweth to his flesh shall of the flesh reap corruption; but he that soweth to the Spirit shall of the Spirit reap life everlasting. And let us not be weary in well doing: for in due season we shall reap, if we faint not."

QUESTIONS CHAPTER 3- SESSION3

1. What are two of the tools that Satan uses to come against God's Saints?

2. If we expect to stand, what is important for us to hold to?

3. What are the five gates that allows Satan an inroad into our lives?

4. Doing what, gives Satan and advantage in our lives?

CHAPTER 4

Love

SESSION 1

AGAPE LOVE/THE GOD KIND OF LOVE

Agape– In the New Testament, the fatherly love of God for humans, as well as the human reciprocal (done in return) love for God: unconditional love.

Love is **patient** – "Able to accept or tolerate delays, problems, or suffering without becoming annoyed or anxious."

Love is **kind** – "Generous, helpful, and caring about others."

Love is **longsuffering** - "Having or showing patience in spite of troubles, especially those caused by others."

Love does not **envy** – "Being discontented longing for someone else's advantages."

Love **Vaunteth** not itself – "Does not boast or talk with excessive pride and self-satisfaction about one's achievements."

Love is not **Puffed up** – "Egocentric, selfish, concerned exclusively with oneself: seeking or concentrating on one's own advantage, pleasure, or well-being without regard for others."

Love doth not **behave itself unseemly** – "Inappropriate behavior."

Love **seeketh not her own** – (being proud) "Showing an excessively high opinion of oneself or own importance."

Love **thinketh no evil** – God forgives and forgets. We also should do the same.

Love is **not easily provoked** – "Deliberately made annoyed or angry."

Love **Rejoiceth not in iniquity, but rejoiceth in the truth** – Doesn't get excited with evil, but rejoiceth with truth.

Love **beareth all things** – Love endures wrong, with a heart of forgiveness and grace.

Love **believeth all things** – Love trusts and looks for the good in others rather than the bad.

Love **hopeth all things** – Optimistically looks for the good only and expects nothing negative.

Love **endureth all things** – Having a mind to endure regardless and never give up (suffer patiently).

Love **never faileth** – "To fade; die away, is always successful and never fall short."

As we see, the meaning of agape love describes the love of God. God's love is so unselfish and a love that compelled him to rescue an undeserving people that were destined to die without any hope of escaping eternal damnation. Let us remember the full extinct of how we were in sin. The bible declares that "the heart of man was only evil continuously." Let us also consider the imagination of man was so deprived and his desire was to bring to pass his thoughts. Man was lost and condemned to a fiery hell! We would like to show you a few examples of the Father's love towards us, his people.

Examples:

(A) Ephesians 2:3-5, states – "Among whom also we all had our conversation in times past in the lusts of our flesh fulfilling the desires of the flesh and of the mind, and were by nature the Children of wrath, even as others. But God, who is rich in mercy, for his great love wherewith he loved us, Even when we were dead in sins, hath quickened us together with Christ, (by grace ye are saved;)"

We can see how God loved sinful mankind, which motivated him to commend his love towards us while we were yet sinners.

(B) Romans 5:8 – "But God commendeth his love toward us, in that, while we were yet sinners, Christ died for us."

In John the third chapter, we are able to see the great love that the Lord has for mankind.

(C) John 3:16 – "For God so loved the world, that he gave his only begotten Son, that whosoever believeth in him should not perish, but have everlasting life." Therefore, we as disciples have been commissioned to (Matthew 10:8)- "heal the sick, cleanse the lepers, raise the dead, cast out devils: freely ye have received, freely give."

I would like to show you three other types of love that are considered to be love, but are not as significant as agape love.

1. Eros – "A passionate love displayed through physical affection."

2. Phileo – "Brotherly love, friendship; kind and generous. It continues to give even when the other is unkind and unworthy."

3. Storge – Family love

QUESTIONS CHAPTER 4 - SESSION 1

1. What is considered to be Agape Love?

2. Why is it important for us to walk in this type of love?

3. Why would this love solve all the problems in the home and In the Church?

4. What is Storge?

SESSION 2

GOD IS LOVE

As Christians, we must have the same attributes as Christ. The book of Matthews the fifth chapter, describes God's attributes within the Beatitudes.

Our first attribute is to be poor in our fleshly and carnal spirit, which will in turn cause us to receive the kingdom of heaven.

Attribute #2 – Shows us the importance of a supplicated prayer as we cry out from our hearts to the Lord, he promises us that we will be comforted.

Attribute #3 – Teaches us that as disciples, we must walk in meekness to be able to receive our earthly promise.

Attribute #4 – Teaches us as disciples, we must hunger and thirst after the things of God and he promised that we will be filled.

Attribute #5 – Teaches us in our endeavor, to walk with God, we must be merciful if we expect to receive mercy. In other words, we must forgive to receive forgiveness. In all, one must realize that you will reap what you have sown.

Attribute #6 – This attribute ensures us that if our heart is pure, that we shall see God. In other words, any bitterness, strife or envy will separate us from God's presence.

Attribute #7 – Teaches us as disciples, that we are called to be peacemakers. This will show the world that we are children of God!

Attribute #8 – This attribute shows how powerful our love must be to endure all types of persecutions, knowing clearly our place in heaven has been assured.

Attribute #9 – Teaches us as disciples, that we are blessed when we are tried, persecuted, talked about and mistreated, because we are fully aware of our reward. We should rejoice!!

As disciples, the Lord is teaching us that we must become like him, walking fully in his spirit of love. The responsibility that is laid upon us to minister and reach the world is utterly impossible without the love of God.

Let us look at 1 John the 4th chapter, where it describes another attribute of God's love. I John 4:7 commands us to love one another and if we are to be of God, we must love one another. It is clearly stated in I John 4:8 that "God is Love." It warns us that if we do not walk in love, that we are not of God and know not God.

One must examine and ask themself "Am I a true child of God, walking in love or am I talking about something that I don't have?"

As disciples, let us consider how Jesus came to empower us and to live through us as we walk in love towards our brethren, never forgetting the love of God towards us as he became the propitiation or payment to get us back into favor with God. We ought to show the same type of love towards mankind, by directing them to Christ.

The importance of us knowing rather Christ is within us, is based upon our acknowledgement of his spirit having active course in our lives. In other words, the attribute of Christ ought to be clearly seen.

My hope as your spiritual teacher, is that you realize how essential walking in Jesus' love and the scripture states. 1 John 4:16 – "And we have known and believed the love that God had to us. God is Love; and he that dwelleth in love dwelleth in God, and God in him." Here again, we will see and understand the importance of the acknowledgment of Christ' love in our lives frees us from the power of being complacent and in turn gives us boldness to fulfill that which God has called us to do.

The Scripture shows us in the fourth chapter, that if we are willing to walk in God's spirit and not in the flesh, "as Christ is so we in this present world." In other words, Ephesians 3:20 – "Now unto him that is able to do exceeding abundantly above all that we ask or think, according to the power that worketh in us," STOP and ask yourself, what can't I do? What can't I achieve?

Please remember that love produces faith, faith produces boldness, boldness eliminates the torment of fear.

The Lord expects us as disciples, to allow the love that was given unto us to compel us to have compassion for those who are lost in sin.

QUESTIONS CHAPTER 4 - SESSION 2

1. Can you give two attributes of the love of God?

2. What should we do when we are persecuted?

3. The lesson tells us that if we don't walk, live and possess something, that we are not a part of Christ. What is that?

4. Why is it important for us to share this love?

SESSION 3

I AM NOT FLESH. I AM SPIRIT, I AM LOVE

As we go through this study, I would like for you to keep in mind Proverbs 23:7 – "For as he thinketh in his heart, so is he:" In other words, if one constantly thinks according to the flesh, filters all decisions through the flesh, motivated and directed by the flesh, of course you are flesh. Remember the scriptures states: Romans 7:18 – "For I know that in me (that is in my flesh) dwelleth no good thing: for to will is present with me; but how to perform that which is good I find not."

Truly as we can see that the scriptures declares that walking in our flesh, that one would become spiritually unprofitable. As we can also see, according to Romans 7:5- "For when we were in the flesh, the motions of sins, which were by the law, did work in our members to bring forth fruit unto death."

We would like for you to remember that you cannot be a child of God in the flesh according to Romans 9:8 – "That is, they which are the children of the flesh, these are not the children of God: but the children of the promise are counted for the seed."

Let us bring this study of the flesh to a conclusion by saying according to I Corinthians 1:26 – "For ye see your calling, brethren, how that not many wise men after the flesh, not many mighty, not many noble, are called," Also I Corinthians 1:29 – "That no flesh should glory in his presence."

I AM SPIRIT

I am spirit, therefore, I realize John 6:63 – "It is the spirit that quickeneth; the flesh profiteth nothing: The words that I speak unto you, they are spirit and they are life."

In the previous segment concerning the flesh, Proverbs 23:7-" For as he thinketh in his heart, so is he," this is why we express strongly that one must think spirit and know that you can't be born again, unless by the spirit and by water according to John 3:5 – "Jesus answered, verily, verily, I say unto thee, Except a man be born of water and of the Spirit, he can not enter into the Kingdom of God." Therefore, my statement is bold and I will not back up from it. I am spirit and I shall worship the Lord in Spirit and in truth according to John 4:24 – "God is a spirit: and they that worship him must worship him in Spirit and in truth". This is why many churches and people are empty and not complete. For the Lord is not searching for them, he's only searching for those that are willing to worship him in spirit and in truth.

I AM LOVE

The Lord has given us a commandment and a strict warning, whereby we may be able to determine rather we are his true disciples.

(A)   John 13:34-35 – "A new commandment I give unto you, that ye love one another; as I have loved you, that ye also love one another. By this shall all men know that ye are my disciples, if ye have love one to another."

(B)   John 14:15 - "If ye love me, keep my commandments"

(C)   John 14:21-22 – "He that hath my commandments, and keepeth them, he it is that loveth me: and he that loveth me shall be loved of my Father, and I will love him, and will manifest myself to him. Judas saith unto him, not Iscariot, Lord, how is it that thou wilt manifest thyself unto us, and not unto the world?"

Remember, we are spirit and we are Love and love is Joy (a feeling of great pleasure and happiness; rejoicing), peace (A state of harmony, quiet or calm that isn't disturbed by anything at all), longsuffering (having or showing patience in spite of troubles, especially those caused by others), gentleness (The quality of kind, tender or mild mannered), goodness (the quality of being morally good or virtuous), faith (complete trust or confidence in someone or something; strong belief in God or in the doctrines rather than proof), meekness (an attitude or quality of heart whereby a person is willing to accept and submit without resistance to the will and desire of someone else) and temperance (moderation in action, thought, or feeling, restraint).

Praise the Lord! One easily can see that love is action, purpose, motivation and a strong directive!

If we are to walk in love, we will whole-heartedly follow Christ. There will be no foolishness in our homes. The Saints will walk in love with no schisms and move to fulfill God's directives upon our lives.

QUESTIONS- CHAPTER 4 - SESSION 3

1. What is our subject? Explain it's meaning in your words.

2. Can you give one example of our flesh, taken from our lesson?

3. I am Spirit. Can you explain who, what, where and why?

4. According to the ending statement in our lesson, explain what it means to walk in love.

CHAPTER 5

The Spirit

SESSION 1

INDWELLING SPIRIT OF GOD

We are about to enter a fascinating study of the spirit, which within itself is miraculous, omniscient (knowing all things), limitless and would take us to the supernatural reaches of who we are in God.

Jesus prayed that we would receive this spirit in John 14:16-17 "And I will pray the Father, and he shall give you another Comforter, that he may abide with you for ever; Even the spirit of truth; whom the world can not receive, because it seeth him not, neither knoweth him: but ye know him; for he dwelleth with you, and shall be in you." John 14:26- "But the comforter, which is the Holy Ghost, whom the Father will send in my name, he shall teach you all things, and bring all things to your remembrance, whatsoever I have said unto you."

The Holy Ghost is not a third person in the Godhead, but rather the spirit of God (the Creator), the Spirit of the resurrected Christ. The Holy Ghost comes to dwell in the hearts and live in everyone who believes and obeys the gospel as the Comforter, Sustainer and Keeper. Salvation consists of deliverance from all sin and unrighteousness through the blood of Jesus Christ.

The New Testament experience of salvation consist of repentance from sin, water baptism of the Holy Ghost, after which the Christian is to live a godly life. Therefore, it is important to always remember that we are a spirit, we live in a body and we have a soul, according to I Thessalonians 5:23. It's important for God's disciples to begin to comprehend the importance of identifying with his being, in which it is his connection with Christ.

It is also important to realize that if we expect to be effective or to achieve the fulfillment of our called purpose, we must totally operate in the spirit. According to Colossians 1:26-27- "Even the mystery which hath been hid from ages and from generations, but now is made manifest to his saints: To whom God would make known what is the riches of the glory of this mystery among the Gentiles; which is Christ in you, the hope of glory."

We clearly see that if we are to be able to walk in the glory of God, it takes one to acknowledge that it is totally God and not ourselves. Paul tells us in II Corinthians 4:7v.- "But we have this treasure in earthen vessels, that the excellency of the power may be of God, and not of us." Ourselves? What is the scripture referring to? It's referring to our bodies, our flesh and our carnal state of mind. This is why the scriptures lets us know that in my flesh dwelleth no good thing. - Romans 7:18v.- "For I know that in me (that is, in my flesh), dwelleth no good thing: for to will is present with me; but how to perform that which is good I find not."

It is our desire to achieve or to do great things in the Lord, but it is impossible walking in the flesh. Through the spirit, God has made us supernatural beings that are able to do or achieve great things. Therefore, we are commanded to walk in the spirit and not the flesh. Romans 8:1v- "There is therefore now no condemnation to them which are in Christ Jesus, who walk not after the flesh, but after the Spirit."

God has empowered his people to accomplish and do mighty things in this world. I John 4:17v.- "Herein is our love made perfect, that we may have boldness in the day of judgment: because as he is, so are we in this world." In the spirit of God, we see that we are not weak, pitiful, sorrowful, nor defeated in no-wise.

The scriptures let us know that "we are the head and not the tail, we are above and not beneath." We are truly able, if we can comprehend that we have the same spirit that raised Jesus from the dead, dwelling in us.

We can see again in the strong admonishment in Romans 8:1v. and 5v., not to walk in flesh, but to walk in the spirit. We have also been told, "they that are in the flesh cannot please God. If you live after the flesh, you shall die: but if you through the deeds of the Spirit do mortify the deeds of the body, you shall live."

These are some examples that we will explain of the beauty of one that has walked in the spirit.

1. By walking in the spirit, I received my sonship
2. The Lord Jesus is my Father (Abba, Father)
3. I am a joint heir with Jesus Christ- Therefore, "if I suffer with him, I will be glorified with him", meaning that I will reign according to Romans 5:17v.-"For if by one man's offense death reigned by one, much more they which receive abundance of grace and of the gift of righteousness shall reign in life by one, Jesus Christ."
4. The spirit helps our infirmities, because as we pray in the spirit, we have direct access to God.

5. Because of our spiritual connection with God, we know that all things work together for good for them who truly love God (obeying his commandments) and the called (have surrendered their will), according to his purpose (a willing mind to fulfill that which God has called one to do).

6. The Lord wants you to realize that you are the called (predetermined, I knew that you would be here), you are the justified (declared or made righteous in the sight of God), you are the glorified (glorious, worthy and one to be honored).

7. We are kept, protected and secured by God. If this is true, then nothing anyone can do or say, that will hurt or stop us from succeeding.

8. We should surely be confident in this fact, that if God loved us with such a great love, that he gave his son, we should never allow ourselves to wonder nor fear how our lives or the fulfillment of our spiritual purpose shall turn out, because the Lord surely has given us all that pertaineth to life.

9. If we are the justified by Christ (they whom have been cleansed as though have never sinned), the condemnation of others shouldn't move or affect us, knowing that it is Christ that purchased our salvation and not man. Also, our confidence and boldness should be in knowing that Jesus Christ rose from the dead and is forever making intercession for us.

This is why it is impossible for anything, rather it be spiritual, natural or any other wise, can stop us from achieving and obtaining anything that we desire to do or go after Christ, according to Romans 8:31- "What shall we then say to these things? If God be for us, who can be against us?"

The Lord truly wants us to be secured in this world by coming to the realization that he is supplying all that we can or will ever need, according to Romans 8:32- "He spared not his own Son but delivered him up for us all, how shall he not with him also freely give us all things?"

The scripture states in Romans 8:33- "Who shall lay anything to the charge of God's elect? It is God that justifieth." The Lord is showing how precious we are as his elect, assuring us that, because the fact that we are justified (declaring that we are righteous in the sight of God), that no one will be able to bring an accusation against us.

In Romans 8:31-37, these scriptures, HALLELUJAH I PRAISE GOD!!! Shows us why the flesh is defeated. Our love for God is intact and there is absolutely nothing that can separate us from this love and "nay, in all these things, we are more than conquerors through him that loved us." (Romans 8:37)

QUESTIONS – CHAPTER 5 – SESSION 1

1. Why do you believe that we are warned not to walk in the flesh?

2. What does it mean by "something is dwelling in me"? What's its purpose? What does it do? Why is it there.

3. In what way does the spirit equip us?

4. Give me two examples of why we should have the Holy Ghost, from the nine examples that were given.

SESSION 2

I WANT, I DESIRE, AND I MUST SEEK AFTER A GIFT

This will be our study of why it is so important for one to desire spiritual gifts according to 1 Corinthians the fourteenth chapter. We are admonished to follow after charity and desire spiritual gifts.

We are hoping that this study will motivate each member to come to the realization that the Lord is calling all of us to become involved. We must see that it is expedient for us to pursue and to seek diligently after a spiritual gift, to be able to help the body. According to 1 Corinthians 12:31v.- "Covet (yearn to possess or have something) But covet earnestly the best gifts: and yet show I unto you a more excellent way." This is a definite call for all of us as Christians to Pursue! Pursue! Pursue! Until we Obtain! Obtain! Obtain!

Let us go into why it is so essential for these spiritual gifts and why they must be effectively working in the house of God. Please understand that there are diversities of gifts in the body, but all this is needed for the proper functioning of the body.

The scripture lets us know that there are differences of administrations (the process or activity of running a business, organization, etc.) Therefore, we understand that there are different gifts, different methods of administration, but truly one spirit. 1 Corinthians 12:6-7V. "And there are diversities of operations, but it is the same God which worketh all in all. But the manifestation of the Spirit is given to every man to profit withal."

If we, as the church, desire or hope to mature, grow, and develop a strong church, I'll say again, that we must obtain spiritual gifts.

The Lord knows that for the body to grow, it will need discipline and structure, to produce such a oneness that will bring about the effectual workings of the Lord among his believers.

Please note that the Lord is not the author of confusion, which means that there cannot be any envy or strife among his people. There must be respect of one's gift according to 1 Corinthians 12:15v.--31v. These scriptures show us the importance of staying in your lane and walking in our gift and no one else's. Not belittling (making someone feel unimportant) anyone else's gift and that each saint have the same respect for one another, if one of us suffer, we all suffer, having the self-same spirit. If one of us honored, blessed or lifted up, then we all are, because there are no big "I's" and no little "You's". We are all the same.

There should be no schism (a split of a group into different sections as a result of a difference in beliefs) in the body; but that the members should have the same care one for another.

Our study now will take us into the gifts and the explanations of them.

- Minister – A minister is told to wait on his ministry. In other words, to be sure of his ministry,
  (A) **Preacher** (B) **Apostle** (C) **Pastor** (D) **Teacher**

Having the responsibility of bringing God's people to spiritual perfection, by using the scriptures "for doctrine, reproof, correction and instruction in righteousness, that the man of God may be perfect, throughly furnished unto all good works." (II Timothy 3:16-17).

- The gift of **exhortation** (the ability to lift and exalt God highly, to encourage, cheer, excite or to give strength)
- The gift of **giving** - The gift of giving works in the heart of a gentle, submissive and humble individual that gives whenever asked or prompted by God. They give from their resources and services. They are truly servants!
- **Rule with diligence** – This speaks on each individual being able to rule themselves well. Performing meticulously (showing detail) in their own actions, realizing that their performance is a part of the greater body. In other words, if I don't perform my job, I hinder the body.
- **Having the gift of mercy**- This is a person who shows pity (the feeling of sorrow and compassion caused by the suffering and misfortune of others), not making an individual or entity pay for the wrong that they have committed, cheerfully and willingly forgiving.

Let us continue on with the gifts of the spirit. These last few gifts that I will show you are considered the major gifts and the major hitters that changes lives, increase ministries and these are what I think that the spirit was speaking of when it says "desire the best gifts" in 1 Corinthians 12:8.

- Word of wisdom- A specific, direct and distinct word that come directly from God, usually given to the one that have this gift for the church or individual.

- Word of knowledge – A gift that is sometimes looked on as a prophet or one that can discern or give knowledge about a person, place or thing.
- Gift of Faith-The gift of faith is Considered a gift that enables the individual to have a high level of spiritual perception of God's word that causes them to easily see the move of God in any matter.
- Gift of healing-Supernatural enablement given to a believer to minister various kinds of healing and restoration to individuals through the power of the Holy Ghost.
- Working of miracles- Examples of the working miracles is when a bolt joining in a fractured bone disappears, or when a missing arm grows or even when money shows up. Situations that have no sensible or reasonable answer.
- Discerning of spirits- This gift is given to all believers, but the gift intensifies as one grows and matures. It is simply the ability to determine righteous or evil spirits (good and evil spirits)
- Diversity of tongues and interpretation of tongues. In two different places of the scriptures, it gives us two types of tongues. One of these tongues is received by all believers after receiving the gift of the Holy Ghost. With this tongue, one is speaking directly unto God. I Corinthians the fourteenth chapter speaks of another type of tongue. Many believe that this tongue is used to communicate with the church by using diversity of tongues as messages to the church. As an one is used in this capacity, they must truly seek the interpretation of the tongue expressed. Therefore, the gift of interpretation is used.

As we can see, these gifts are placed in the body to make the body strong and increase in size.

QUESTIONS-CHAPTER 5 – SESSION 2

1. Why is it so important for each member to have all things common?

2. We understand that the Lord is the giver of the gifts through the spirit. What are the specific reasons that the gifts are given?

3. What is the gift of exhortation?

4. What is the gift of the word of wisdom?

5. Why do you think that we are encouraged to covet the best gifts?

SESSION 3

SPIRITUAL WARFARE

In this study, we will learn why we have been empowered to defeat all spiritual and natural entities that may come against us.

First of all, the scripture declares that we shall receive power after that the Holy Ghost is come upon us, giving us power to be witnesses throughout the world. The Lord has given us power against unclean spirits, to cast them out, to heal all manner of sickness and all manner of disease, according to Matthew 10:1. I truly wonder rather we have come to the realization that we all have been given such power to use to build up the kingdom of God.

The Lord re-emphasized in the book of Mark, that "we have power to heal sicknesses, and to cast out devils." The book of Mark also states that we "have been given power over unclean spirits" (A wicked spirit; a demon).

In the fourth chapter of the book of Luke, the Lord is showing us the method whereby we should be able to take authority over all unclean spirits by doing what he did in Luke 4:36- "And they were all amazed, and spake among themselves, saying, What a word is this! For with authority and power he commandeth the unclean spirits, and they come out."

The Lord is showing us that by walking in the supernatural, not in the flesh, according to Luke 10:17-19vs.- "And the seventy returned again with joy, saying, Lord, even the devils are subject unto us through thy name. And he said unto them, I beheld Satan as lightning fall from heaven. Behold, I give unto you power to tread on serpents and scorpions, and over all the power of the enemy: and nothing shall by any means hurt you."

The Lord has truly empowered the saints of God, the true believers, letting us know that according to John 14:12-13- "Verily, verily, I say unto you, he that believeth on me, the works that I do shall he do also; and greater works than these shall he do; because I go unto my Father. And whatsoever ye shall ask in my name, that will I do, that the Father may be glorified in the Son."

In the book of Acts, this power is demonstrated by Stephen in Acts 6:8- "And Stephen, full of faith and power, did great wonders and miracles among the people." We can also be effective in changing people lives by operating in the same spirit.

We will conclude the portion of this study with Ephesians 3:20- "Now unto him that is able to do exceeding abundantly above all that we ask or think, according to the power that worketh in us."

As disciples, we waste our time walking, being controlled by or fighting against anyone or anything in the flesh. It is truly defective and destructive to our spiritual walk with Christ.

It is important for us to remember John 4:23-24 "But the hour cometh, and now is, when the true worshippers shall worship the Father in spirit and in truth: for the Father seeketh such to worship him, God is a Spirit: and they that worship him must worship him in spirit and in truth." Also, remember John 6:63v- "It is the spirit that quickeneth; the flesh profiteth nothing: the words that I speak unto you, they are spirit, and they are life."

Operating in the flesh is the same method as the children of Israel walking in the wilderness, depending on and looking to their flesh, getting nowhere fast. Therefore, we are commanded to war in the spirit and not in the flesh according to Ephesians 6:12v.- "For we wrestle not against flesh and blood, but against spiritual wickedness in high places."

The battle is real and is one that is fought daily. This is why we have been instructed as it states in Ephesians 6:13v.-14v "Wherefore take unto you the whole armour of God, that ye may be able to withstand in the evil day, and having done all, to stand. Stand therefore, having your loins girt about with truth, and having on the breastplate of righteousness;"

- We must love the truth for one to be strong in the Spirit. Thessalonians tells us that "the devil comes with all deceivableness and lying wonders," deceiving those who love not the truth.
- The breastplate which is part of our spiritual armour, covers essential parts. Our heart, which is where the issues of life flows.
- We are commanded to keep our feet covered in the word, meaning to let God's word direct and guide us and by doing so, the peace of God will fill our lives.
- The shield of faith is the part of the armour that shields us from the fiery dots of Satan.
- The scripture tells us to "let this mind be in us which was also in Christ Jesus," instructing us by this part of the armour, which is the helmet, informs us that

it is essential for us to know that we are saved, full of the Holy Ghost, free from sin and standing in the power of our salvation.

- The sword of the spirit is what I consider the most important part of our armour, because it is the word of God.

I must present to you that "our weapons are mighty through God to the pulling down of strong holds; Casting down imaginations, and every high thing that exalteth itself against the knowledge of God, and bringing into captivity every thought to the obedience of Christ;" (II Corinthians 10:5)

QUESTIONS CHAPTER 5-SESSION 3

1. What is the source of our power and where did it come from?

2. What are three uses of this power?

3. Explain to me how one can walk consistently in this power.

4. What are 4 weapons that we have through putting on the whole armour?

CHAPTER 6

The Law vs. Grace

SESSION 1

LAW

In our first study, to appreciate grace, let's get a simple understanding of the law and its severity.

According to John 1:17- "For the law was given by Moses, but grace and truth came by Jesus Christ."

In the book of Exodus, we would like to show you the benefits that the Lord promised to his people if they would follow after his given laws and keep it (which is over 631 different laws).

The Lord promised in Exodus "If thou wilt diligently hearken to the voice of the Lord thy God, and wilt do that which is right in his sight, and wilt give ear to his commandments and keep all his statutes, I will put none of these disease upon thee which I have brought upon the Egyptians: for I am the Lord that healeth thee."

The Lord is striving to get his people totally dependent upon him and his word as the similar promise in Deuteronomy 28:1-2- "And it shall come to pass, if thou shalt hearken diligently unto the voice of the Lord thy God, to observe and to do all his commandments which I command thee this day, that the Lord thy God will set thee on high above all nations of the earth: And all these blessings shall come on thee, and over take thee, if thou shalt hearken unto the voice of the Lord thy God." Also, "Blessed in the city, field, by the fruit of thy body, thy ground, the fruit of thy cattle, blessed will be thy basket and store, blessed when thou goest in and out, when thy enemies rise up against thee, they shall come against thee one way and flee seven ways."

The Lord will command his blessings upon you and bless all that you set your hands to do. The Lord will bless you in your neighborhood and all your surroundings, he will also establish his people holy unto himself, if thou shalt keep the commandments of the Lord thy God and walk in his ways.

One may say "What great benefits and promises that the Lord has promised us, if we keep the law!" The promises are great, but the problem is our ability to follow the law and the consequences if we fail. The penalty for not walking according to the law is death and there is no pardons.

In the same chapter, The Lord reveals to us the curses that will fall upon any individual that fails to walk faithfully after the law. Deuteronomy 28:15- "But it shall come to pass, if thou wilt not hearken unto the voice of the Lord thy God, to observe to do all his commandments and his statutes which I command thee this day; that all these curses shall come upon thee, and overtake thee:"

In the book of Exodus chapter 24:12, the Lord commanded Moses to come upon the mountains where he would give him tables of the law, in which he is commanded to teach the people.

The Lord God, our Master, has always wanted a people that was separate from the world, who walked according to Holy ordinances and laws which are stated in Deuteronomy 4:8- "And what nation is there so great, that hath statutes and judgments so righteous as all this law, which I set before you this day?"

I can't emphasize strongly enough, that there are more than 631 laws that one must follow. Therefore, there are more than 631 opportunities of one falling under the curse or being put to death.

Let's stop here. I don't want anyone to get the wrong idea. According to Romans the seventh chapter, the law is holy. Romans 7:12- "Wherefore the law is holy and the commandment holy, and just, and good." Romans 7:7-9- "What shall we say then? Is the law sin? God forbid. Nay, I had not known sin, but by the law: for I had not known lust, except the law had said, thou shalt not covet. But sin, taking occasion by the commandment, wrought in me all manner of concupiscence (man sinning willingly). For without the law sin was dead. For I was alive without the law once: but when the commandment came, sin revived, and I died."

Before the law, man was a law unto himself, feeling somewhat justified in doing whatever he thought to be right or wrong. In that the law came, it revealed unto man how sinful and lost he really is. Therefore, out of desperation, man proclaimed in Romans 7:24- "O wretched man that I am! Who shall deliver me from the body of this death?"

GRACE

As we are able to see in the book of John 1:14- "And the Word was made flesh, and dwelt among us, (and we beheld his glory, the glory as of the only begotten of the Father,) full of grace and truth." Also, that grace we received - John 1:16-17- And of his fulness have all we received, and grace for grace. For the law was given by Moses, but grace and truth came by Jesus Christ."

You might ask the question, "What then is grace?" Grace is God's unmerited (not earned nor deserved) favor (an act of kindness beyond what is due). It is also God's ability (God's effectual workings in one's life enabling us to do that which we would not have been able to do without him), anointing (the supernatural power of God giving us the power to function effectively in the spiritual realm) and power (grace has empowered us to have and live according to the righteousness of God). All of these are actively at work in our lives.

Grace sounds to be great! How can one receive this grace? I'm glad that you asked! Grace comes after one receives salvation for their soul. The Scripture declares that "we are saved by grace through faith and that not of yourselves: it is the gift of God," according to Ephesians 2:8. We

see then, that we are saved by grace, therefore this should compel one to desire more grace within their lives.

According to the book of James, we are instructed, that if we desire more grace, we must humble ourselves (James 4:6).

It is a truth that God resisteth the proud and gives grace unto the humble. Therefore, one would need to humble himself if it is truly his desire to receive more grace.

In the Book of Hebrews 7:19, The scripture shows us how that the law could not make us perfect, but the coming in of Jesus Christ under the new covenant, which is his grace (giving us what we don't deserve), brings us to perfection.

Hebrews 7:22- "By so much was Jesus made a surety of a better testament." This new covenant or testament is showing God's grace toward us according to Hebrews 7:25- "Wherefore he is able also to save them to the uttermost that come unto God by him, seeing he ever liveth to make intercession for them."

In Hebrews the tenth chapter and the third verse, we can see how, that by the law, man yearly had to be forgiven, but here we see in Hebrews 8:12- "For I will be merciful to their unrighteousness, and their sins and their iniquities will I remember no more."

As we can clearly see, Christ has completely secured our place in glory according to Hebrews 9:26-27- "For then must he often have suffered since the foundation of the world: but now once in the end of the world hath he appeared to put away sin by the sacrifice of himself. And as it is appointed unto men once to die, but after this the judgment:"

As we come to the end of this study of Law vs. Grace, it is a fact that man was lost, defeated, deceived and felt completely helpless to his own carnal desires. The Lord Jesus decided to show forth his grace toward all mankind by leaving glory, setting aside his deity, wrapping himself up in flesh, being born of a virgin, he came to save us from sin and our predicament by being an example of how to live Holy in this present world. He was tempted and tried in the flesh, but did not submit or succumb to sin.

As we begin to show you the things that he endured, please realize that these are the things that we should have endured for the wrong that we have done. He was judged by unjust judges, lied on by wicked witnesses, slapped, beaten unrecognizably, then judged to be put to death with such a brutal death. They whipped his back, scourging him with a whip that snatched flesh from his body, they then made him carry, a rugged cross. Keep in mind that they constantly tormented him, ridiculing him, joking and jesting against him. As they reached skull hill, he was laid upon the cross where large spikes were hammered into his hands. One foot was placed upon the other, where they were fastened to the cross. The cross was then raised, where Christ became the Lamb, the blood sacrifice, the payment, the propitiation for all of our sins. This shows you the real meaning of what one doesn't deserve, given freely by our Savior. Yes! Yes! This is Grace!

QUESTIONS – CHAPTER 6 -SESSION 1

1. Why was the law given?

2. Knowing the meaning of dispensation, what dispensation was this, when the law was given?

3. What was the penalty for breaking the law?

4. In this lesson, what must one be to obtain grace?

SESSION 2

BY GRACE WE HAVE OBTAINED ALL THAT WE NEED

KEY VERSE: 2 PETER 1:3- "According as His Divine Power Hath Given Us All Things That Pertain Unto Life And Godliness, Through The Knowledge Of Him That Hath Called Us To Glory And Virtue:"

We will start this study off with a reminder of the utter failure of man and his lack of ability to do anything right, according to the things of God, without the presence of God. Simply stated, man needs God's grace to be saved, to live save, to love others, to achieve or obtain any great success in the things of God.

The book of Romans 5:2-declares "By whom also we have access by faith into this grace wherein we stand, and rejoice in hope of the glory of God."

I hope that you truly understand the magnitude of what this verse is saying! It is telling us that we can move from dreaming about greatness, talking about achieving greatness or even pondering on how one can do something great.

The Lord, by his grace which has been given unto us, truly has enabled us to live and occupy in the supernatural, spiritual realm. In other words, where we will freely begin to see, by the grace of God, the impossible made possible and that which couldn't be, begin to be.

Psalms 84:11- "For the Lord God is a sun and shield: the Lord will give grace and glory: No good thing will he withhold from them that walk uprightly." The Lord has promised in the scripture, not to withhold any good thing from us. I am hoping that we will realize that by faith, what we truly have access to by grace.

By grace, the Lord lets us know that we have abundance of his grace (unmerited, undeserved goodness) and he has made us righteous, which in turn, we are able to say that we are the righteousness of God.

We are encouraged to abide faithfully in the grace that has been given unto us, and that this grace would enable us to be stedfast in the gospel, according to Acts 13:43.

We may have wondered, because of being a sister or brother, how can I continue or take part in this gospel? Remember, if you believe in what God has given you, proof or signs and wonders will follow after the believer, according to Acts 14:3.

We have truly been equipped by the Lord to do great things in the Kingdom. The enemy is on the attack to hinder and stop the ministry. This ministry of grace, which is teaching people that the Lord has truly given us power over anything that will try to defeat us, must be proclaimed and the enemy is out to try and stop it. We (the Saints of God), must declare as Paul did in Acts 20:24 -"But none of these things move me, neither count I my life dear unto myself, so that I might finish my course with joy, and the ministry, which I have received of the Lord Jesus, to testify the gospel of the grace of God."

We are assured that this grace that we have access to by faith according Acts 20:32- "And now, Brethren, I commend you to God, and to the word of his grace which is able to build you up, and to give you an inheritance among all them which are sanctified." Therefore, we can clearly see that the grace of God enables us to fulfill what he has called us to do here upon the earth. This is why you hear Paul state, that "by the grace of God, I've been made an Apostle and by God's grace, I was sent to the gentiles." We should be able to say that "By God's grace, he has enabled me to do __ or __ or even __." You can fill in the blanks.

In 1 Corinthians 3:10, Paul is letting us know that, by the grace of God, he has spiritually built and established different Christians, because the Lord has made him a master builder and spiritual instructor.

The grace of God is so spectacular, that it makes us inexcusable. If we get out of the flesh and allow God's grace to work within us, God will make us truly effective in our particular part of the body as Paul declared in 1 Corinthians 15:10- "But by the grace of God I am what I am: and his grace which was bestowed upon me was not in vain; but I laboured more abundantly than they all: yet not I, but the grace of God which was with me." You see, grace is a motivator, showing you that the grace in you ought to compel you.

My fellow disciples, we have been given this grace to enable us to accomplish greatness in the Kingdom. If we do nothing with it, seeing that we have it in abundance, II Corinthians 6:1 declares not to have this grace in vain.

As we continue on studying this lesson about grace, we have been admonished by II Corinthians the eighth chapter, to dwell (to stay there, live there) it is referring to the grace of God.

In 1 Peter the fifth Chapter, Peter is telling us that to be able to dwell in grace, one would have to stay humble because, "God resisteth the proud and give grace to the humble," according to 1 Peter 5:5.

You may ask, "What is being proud?" Pride is having a high regard of one's self achievements, accomplishments, one's self-worth or feeling a spirit of greatness above others.

The Lord is instructing us, that if we want to walk in his grace, we would need to submit to that which is needed to make us what we cannot make ourselves.

Please remember, we are sheep and the Lord is our Shepherd and by his grace, he is telling us to humble ourselves and cast all of our cares upon him.

The Lord is encouraging us to be sober (not to be under the influence of another spirit, but subject unto the righteous spirit of God). We are also told to be vigilant (always aware of danger or evil). The reason for this, is that the devil is as a roaring lion seeking whom he may devour.

The Lord is the Lord of all grace, that as you begin to transform, he would stablish (achieve permanent acceptance), strengthen (to make strong), settle (resolving all confusion) you.

1 Peter 5:11- "To him be glory and dominion forever and ever. Amen."

QUESTIONS-CHAPTER 6-SESSION 2

1. What method is used to gain entry into grace?

2. Why do you think that grace introduces us to the supernatural?

3. Why do the lesson states that grace enables one?

4. Why are we instructed to stay under the hand of God?

SESSION 3

HE MUST INCREASE: BUT I MUST DECREASE

KEY VERSE: "Serving the Lord with all humility of mind, and with many tears, and temptations, which befell me by the lying in wait of the Jews:" (Acts 20:19)

In this study of *grace*, we will truly come to the understanding that the Lord desires to do great and magnificent things in the believer's life, making him bold and fearless as he walks before the Lord.

Please indulge with me as I bring a familiar poem:

Footprints

"**O**ne night a man had a dream. He dreamed he was walking along the beach with the LORD. Across the sky flashed scenes from his life. For each scene, he noticed two sets of footprints in the sand, one belonged to him, and the other to the LORD."

"**W**hen the last scene of his life flashed before him, he looked back at the footprints in the sand. He noticed that many times along the path of his life there was only one set of footprints. He also noticed that it happened at the very lowest and saddest times in his life."

"**T**his really bothered him and he questioned the LORD about it. LORD, you said that once I decided to follow you, you'd walk with me, all the way. But I have noticed that during the most troublesome times in my life, there is only one set of footprints. I don't understand why when I needed you most you would leave me."

The LORD replied, "My precious, precious child. I love you and I would never leave you. during your times of trial and suffering, when you see only one set of footprints, it was then that I carried you."

In the poem, we can see that the thoughts of this person caused them to react in the wrong way and a lot of times we find ourselves responding to situations in the same way. The Lord constantly reminds us that it is not us, but it is him, and that no flesh will glory in his presence.

The character in the poem declared that things are hard, where is God? he left me all alone. The response was, I never left you, I'm carrying your burdens and it never was you at any time.

For a moment, I would like for you to travel within your mind and take a glimpse of the individual that you once were, before you were save. Remember how lost you were, disgusted, aggravated and felt shame to the things that you badly wanted to be out of your life, just as the children of Israel felt under the bondage of the Egyptians? Grace came in and delivered them with a mighty hand. Afterwards, feeling the joy of walking out of Egypt as freed men and women, here comes the bitterness of what they had left behind, coming strongly to pull them back into the discuss that they had just left out of.

The spirit of helplessness and hopelessness began to rise again, but praise be to God, grace rose up with a message stating that the enemy you see today, you will see no more forever!

I truly would like for you to see the sheer bitterness of being again and again under the power of the flesh and trust in the grace (what is not deserved) of God to do what you obviously cannot do.

The scripture in the book of Philippians 4:12-13- "I know both how to be abased, and I know how to abound: every where and in all things I am instructed both to be full and to be hungry, both to abound and to suffer need. I can do all things through Christ which strengtheneth me." I can do it! I can obtain it! I can accomplish it and I can achieve it, because it is not the flesh: it is the grace of God!

Can anyone tell me? (Please think strong and hard) What can't I do? What can't I achieve? What can't I accomplish, if I'm totally looking to him that enables me, empowers me and transcend me to the supernatural?

The book of II Corinthians 4:15-18- "For all things are for your sakes, that the abundant grace might through the thanksgiving of many redound to the glory of God. for which cause we faint not; but though our outward man perish, yet the inward man is renewed day by day. For our light affliction, which is but for a moment, worketh for us a far more exceeding and eternal weight of glory; While we look not at the things which are seen, but at the things which are not seen: for the things which are seen are temporal; but the things which are not seen are eternal."

I would like to remind you once again, that our greatest hinderance from spiritual greatness is our flesh, according to Psalm 78:39-40- "For he remembered that they were but flesh; a wind that passeth away, and cometh not again. How oft did they provoke him in the wilderness, and grieve him in the desert!

If we as Holy Ghost filled, royal beings of Christ, don't realize what we have in having access to the grace of God, we will fall into the same trap as the children of Israel. "Yea, they turned back and tempted God, and limited the Holy One of Israel." (Psalm 78:41)

As we come to the conclusion of this third session, I would like for you as disciples to realize, as you look back over Chapter 1, Chapter 2, Chapter 3, Chapter 4, Chapter 5 and even Chapter 6, according to II Corinthians 9:8 - "And God is able to make all grace abound (exist in large numbers) towards you; that ye always having all sufficiency (adequate amount) in all things may abound to every good work:" Therefore, from this day on and evermore, never allow the words "I can't do it" "It's too hard" and "It seems impossible" to come out of your mouth, because it was not you doing it, it was the grace of God doing it all the time!

QUESTIONS

1. What does it mean by He must increase, but I must decrease?

2. How could I serve the Lord with humility of mind? Explain please.

3. How can one rest in the fact that it is the grace of God that is doing it and not themselves?

4. As I read the story of the children of Israel coming out of Egypt, the hopelessness, despair and seeing God's grace delivering them, how many times have this happened to me? Please give a short testimony.

5. In our conclusion of the lesson, we are told that grace abound and is sufficient, can you elaborate?

CHAPTER 7

Faith

SESSION 1

WITHOUT FAITH, IT IS IMPOSSIBLE TO PLEASE GOD

What is faith? Did you know that without faith, it is impossible to please God? Did you know that anything done without faith is sin? Did you also know that without faith, one cannot receive salvation, healing, deliverance and not even the ability to enter into eternal life? Therefore, one who is reading these questions might come to the reasonable conclusion that faith is essential.

We will strive to take each one of these questions and answer them to the hope that your understanding will be enlightened on faith.

1. What is faith? I would like to start by telling you that the bible explains faith to be **"Now** - (meaning right now; present. In other words, I'm seeing it occur while I'm yet speaking) **Faith is the substance** (the ultimate reality that underlines all outward manifestation and change) **of things hoped for** (wanted and expected) **the evidence** (the title deed; the available body of facts or information dictating whether a belief or proposition is true or valid) **of things not seen"** (invisible; no proof or evidence of something which is physical or existing).

Faith shows something else is true or exist; complete trust or confidence in someone or something; strong belief in God or in the doctrine of his word, based on spiritual understanding rather than proof.

We have given you the meaning of what faith is. Now, I would like to give an example of faith in action in the book of Saint John, the eleventh chapter, the first through the forty-ninth verse. At a later, time, you can read it in the entirety, but now, I will abbreviate it. There was a man by the name of Lazarus who became very ill. His sisters then sent for Jesus, that he would come to heal Lazarus. The Lord Jesus, delayed his coming not arriving until Lazarus had been dead for four days. The sisters hope and confidence was in Jesus' coming while Lazarus was sick but, after Lazarus died, all substance and confidence died with him, according to Martha. The Lord striving to ignite Martha's faith, in that which she couldn't see, he proclaimed unto her that he raise the dead by declaring that he is the resurrection. The Lord walking into his "Now faith," which is action, wanted to know where did you bury him! (Please remember that faith is the evidence or proof of that which is not seen) Martha still holding on to that which could be seen or evidence of that which can be seen, declared unto the resurrection (Jesus) that her brother now stinketh; being dead now for four days. The resurrection (Jesus) proclaimed unto her, John 11:40 – "Jesus saith unto her, Said I not unto thee, that, if thou wouldest believe, thou shouldest see the glory of God?"

This is why it is imperative (of vital importance; crucial) for us as disciples to know what faith is.

2. Did you know that without faith, it is impossible to please God? The word declares that he that cometh to God must believe that he is and that he is a rewarder of them that diligently seek him. In other words, the Lord is letting us know that when one come to him, that he must believe that God is able to take care of the situation that he's praying for.

In the book of Numbers, the thirteenth chapter, the twenty-ninth verse through the thirty-third verse and Numbers the entire fourteenth chapter. Again, I will ask that you would read these in their entirety, but I would briefly go over them.

The children of Israel were only a few days from receiving their promise. Due to the lack of faith and having totally, the wrong perspectives, focusing on their inability and not on the power of the promised word of God. God's people considered themselves as grasshoppers, their enemy as giants and the land unconquerable.

The Lord declared, "my glory will be seen throughout the earth and due to your lack of faith, ten different times I showed you my great wonders, but yet, your faith has not grown, and where boldness should be, you are defeated. Therefore. You will not enter into my promise."

Disciples of the Lord, we see that without faith it is impossible to please God, because he that cometh to God, must believe that God is whom he declares himself to be.

In this life, we suffer and will suffer many adversities, circumstances and situations that we will need a good understanding on how to walk in faith. Matthew 13:58- "And he did not many mighty works there because of their unbelief." Without faith, it is impossible to please God!

3. Did you know that anything done without faith is sin? According to Romans 14:23- "And he that doubteth is damned if he eat, because he eateth not of faith: for whatsoever is not of faith is sin."

The scripture explains to us that if I'm singing, testifying, coming to church, preaching or anything that I may be doing, I'm doing it not because I believe it to be right, but

I'm doing it to please others and don't believe that I'm doing it because it is right. We see an example of this in the book of Galatians 2:11-16, where if one walks by flesh, he will not show forth faith.

In our study of faith, hopefully you will see the importance of disciples walking by faith. You may have asked yourself, "How can one obtain faith?" According to Romans 10:17- "So then faith cometh by hearing, and hearing by the word of God." Once one hears the word, please remember that the hearing that we are referring to, is the word being heard by the ears of one's heart.

The scripture tells us in the book of Proverbs 23:7- "For as he thinketh in his heart, so is he: Eat and drink, saith he to thee; but his heart is not with thee." Hopefully, you can clearly see how faith comes. Hearing from our heart produce, and speaking to faith (which is a servant), brings about results.

We see this when the disciples asked the Lord to increase their faith. Luke 17:5-9- "And the apostles said unto the Lord, Increase our faith. And the Lord said, If ye had faith as a grain of mustard seed, ye might say unto this sycamine tree, Be thou plucked up by the root and be thou planted in the sea; and it should obey you. But which of you, having a servant plowing or feeding cattle, will say unto him by and by, when he is come from the field, Go and sit down to meat? And will not rather say unto him, Make ready wherewith I may sup, and gird thyself, and serve me, till I have eaten and drunken; and afterward thou shalt eat and drink? Doth he thank that servant because he did the things that were commanded him? I trow not." As you can see, faith is a servant, so I commend you to command or speak to faith and hold him (faith) to it until the job is complete.

I would like to show you an example where a sinner understood how faith works so much so, that the Lord declared that "never have I seen such great faith, no not in Israel." This man stated unto the Lord that it was no need to come to his house to pray for his servant, but "speak the word only."

This is the example that he proclaimed: Matthew 8:9-10- "For I am a man under authority, having soldiers under me: and I say to this man, Go, and he goeth; and to another, Come, and he cometh and to my servant, Do this, and he doeth it. When Jesus heard it, he marvelled, and said to them that followed, Verily I say unto you, I have not found so great faith, no, not in Israel."

Faith is our servant that enables disciples to walk in the supernatural, doing the impossible!

QUESTIONS

1. What is Faith?

2. Why is it, that without faith, it is impossible to please God?

3. Why is it, that if I do something and do it not by faith, I'm sinning?

4. Faith, is it truly a servant? Why? How?

SESSION 2

A FAITH THAT MOVES MOUNTAINS

This lesson wants one to believe that the mountains of life are removable. In other words, there is absolutely no situation that renders the believer helpless, hopeless, and stuck in any situation that may seem that there's no solution. This study should be called the mountain remover.

Let us go to Mark 11:14. Peter beheld Jesus cursing a fig tree from its roots, demanding that it bring forth no more figs. On the next day, coming to where the fig tree was, to Peter's amazement, the fig tree had obeyed the voice of God and had dried up from the roots.

I believe that mountain moving faith, is a faith that brings one from what we believe to be natural occurrences to accepting the fact that the supernatural is possible. Peter exclaimed; "this is the tree that you cursed!" Jesus responded with no amazement, (just as one that expected it and knew that it would occur as it did). The Lord told Peter to "have faith in God." In other words, believe that you also could've spoken to the fig tree and it would have obeyed you.

Please let us note that the Lord is saying that we have the faith of God or a faith that would move like God, according to Romans 12:3v. "God has given us all *the measure of faith*". The scripture is letting us know that each believer has the measure of faith given by God. It is truly up to us, how we develop it and make it strong. We have also been assured in Galatians 5:22, that each one of us have faith given unto us by the almighty creator. It is our job to develop such faith, to the place where the mountains in our lives are freely moved.

So many times, in one's life, we are spending so much negative energy murmuring and grumbling in detail about our mountains. Proverbs 18:21- "Death and life are in the power of the tongue: and they that love it shall eat the fruit thereof."

We, as disciples of Christ need to begin to utilize our mountain moving faith and tell them (our mountain) where they must go, according to Mark 11:23- "For verily I say unto you, That whosoever shall say unto this mountain, Be thou removed, and be thou cast into the sea; and shall not doubt in his heart, but shall believe that those things which he saith shall come to pass; he shall have whatsoever he saith."

I'm wondering if any of us are willing to do what it is going to take to be a mountain mover. If you are, boldly declare this verse as this <u>Your name</u> shall say unto this mountain (something unmovable, stubborn, impossible) be thou removed (completely out of your life, totally from your surroundings) and be thou cast into the sea; and shall not doubt in his heart; but shall believe that those things (mountains) which <u>Your name</u> saith shall come to pass; (now faith) <u>Your name</u> shall have whatsoever (mountains) <u>Your name</u> saith. Here in this scripture, the Lord is letting us know that he has empowered us. We must realize the authority and power that we have been given in our ability to speak or say to any situation.

The Lord is also letting us know in Mark 11:24, how powerful he is willing to move on our desires. Mark 11:24- "Therefore I say unto you, What things soever ye desire, then ye pray, believe that ye receive them, and ye shall have them."

Hopefully now, we, as disciples realize that such a great faith is given to all disciples, from the lay members, choir members, ushers, mothers, deacons, ministers and the pastors. All should be able to fluently walk in such faith. I would not have you ignorant my brother. There are certain attitudes or certain behaviors that would hinder our faith from flowing (working).

1. According to Mark 11:25-26 - (we must forgive) -But if ye do not forgive, neither will your Father which is in heaven forgive your trespasses.

It is essential that we, as disciples, forgive and never hold anything in our heart against anyone, because our hearts must be clear if we're going to be able to believe from our hearts and freely speak to mountains from our heart.

2. We cannot doubt nor have fear. In other words, no matter how dreadful or overbearing things may seem, we cannot allow our eyes to be removed from off of Christ nor our faith to be shaken.

In Matthew 14:30-31 - "But when he saw the wind boisterous, he was afraid; and beginning to sink, he cried, saying, Lord, save me. And immediately Jesus stretched forth his hand and caught him, and said Unto him, O thou of little faith, wherefore didst thou doubt?" According to Matthew 17:17-20- "Then Jesus answered and said, O faithless and perverse generation, how long shall I suffer you? Bring him hither to me. And Jesus rebuked the devil; and he departed out of him: and the child was cured from that very hour. Then came the disciples to Jesus apart, and said, Why could not we cast him out? And Jesus said unto them, Because of your unbelief: for verily I say unto you, If ye have faith as a grain of mustard seed, ye shall say unto this mountain, Remove hence to yonder place; and it shall remove; and nothing shall be impossible unto you."

After reading these scriptures, there is a profound fact and that should be at the center of your minds, and that is, the Lord didn't and never will tolerate unbelief. Yes! Yes! The Lord expects for all of us to have faith that would remove mountains. He knows that he has done great wonders, miraculous events and he has blessed us to where we know that there were no coincidences. The Lord expects for us to fast, pray and stay in the word, so that our faith becomes unshakeable.

As we come to the conclusion of our lesson on moving mountains, the Lord's message to us is simple. According to Matthew 21:21 - "Jesus answered and said unto them, Verily I say unto you, If ye have faith, and doubt not, ye shall not only do this which is done to the fig tree, but also if ye shall say unto this mountain, Be thou removed, and be thou cast Into the sea; it shall be done." **And that's all I have to say about that!**

QUESTIONS

1. Understanding our subject, mountain remover, why should this cause me to believe that there is no circumstances or situations that can prevent me from achieving or obtaining?

2. How do you believe Proverbs 18:21 ties into this particular lesson:

3. What certain attitudes would hinder mountain moving faith to be active in our lives?

4. What do our lesson tells us that the Lord will totally not tolerate?

SESSION 3

A FAITH THAT OVERCOMES THE WORLD

As we now continue our study on the power of faith, we would like to hopefully open up your eyes to the fact that earth cannot produce, Satan cannot come up with any device that your faith can't overcome.

There's certain characters or habits that one must possess if they desire to always, not sometimes, but always have a faith that will conquer all. Characteristics and habits are learned behaviors that has become a part of our very being. In other words, this behavior has become us. Example: As in the caterpillar moving through the process of metamorphoses, changing from caterpillar to butterfly. When the caterpillar is no longer a caterpillar, but now a butterfly, all of the characteristics and behavior as when he was a caterpillar no longer exist. He has taken on the characteristics of the butterfly. Same as an unbeliever leaving that which is a faithless individual, now becoming a believer taking on now the characteristics as one of faith, never going back to the characteristics of an unbeliever, only pursuing and walking daily in the characteristics of one that has faith.

Our metamorphous is one that have presented his body wholly unto the Lord, separating from his fleshly and carnal ways, being not conformed to that worldly lifestyle, but has transcended to a spiritual lust for the gospel, as we would see here in Romans 1:16-17 - "For I am not ashamed of the gospel of Christ: for it is the power of God unto salvation to everyone that believeth; to the Jew first, and also to the Greek. For therein is the righteousness of God revealed from faith to faith: as it is written, The just shall live by faith." Therefore, it is essential for God's people to love and to have a personal relationship with God's word, consistently moving from faith to faith. In other words, the faith that I use for problem "A" I should be using for problem B C and D. For as you can see, the just (the justified) walk by faith.

Before we continue on, the Lord warned us against holding the truth in ungodliness. In other words, testifying of one thing, but living a totally ungodly life, causing us to be powerless instead of powerful. This is why so many churches are going around in circles instead of seeing the word of God being fulfilled within the walls of the church.

The word of God, here in the book of Romans, tells us clearly that all excuses have been taken completely away from the believer. All of us know and have seen the invisible hand of God working in all that exist and all of that which we know, even to his miraculous hands upon our own lives. There is truly no reason for us not to walk in a faith that overcomes the world. You will find this in Romans 1:17-20.

In the upper part of our lesson, we gave to you a warning and I feel it necessary to warn you again. If we are not persistent, moving from faith to faith, honoring God for who he is and what he showed himself to be, we will become carnal, vain walking away from the light, falling into darkness (sin) honoring more so, the creature rather than our almighty creator. You can find this in Romans 1:21-23.

Precious Saints, as we were saying earlier, about one's characteristics, meaning a behavior that has become a part of said individual, the scripture lets us know that we always triumph (achieve a victory; be successful). This is who we are regardless of what we feel or what we see, according to II Corinthians 2:14.

It is in our ability to forget about ourselves or our flesh and to realize because of the promises of God, we all have a faith in God which overcomes the world. You will find this in II Corinthians 1:20- "For all the promises of God in him are yea, and in him Amen, unto the glory of God by us."

The Lord is saying yes to your healing, deliverance, your breakthroughs and prosperities, yes to all the promises that he has promised us, the believers. So, tell me quickly, before you think too long. If one believes the word of God, how can he not, seeing these great promises, overcome the world? Well, according to the book of Hebrews, the sixth chapter, God promises are sure. Hebrews 6:13-14- "For when God made promise to Abraham, because he could swear by no greater, he swear by himself, Saying Surely blessing I will bless thee, and multiplying I will multiply thee."

As you read these scriptures and hear how important it is to God, for us to believe his promises, as the word declares in Hebrews that God cannot lie, Hebrews 6:18- "That by two immutable things, in which it was impossible for God to lie, we might have a strong consolation, who have fled for refuge to lay hold upon the hope set before us:"

It is important to realize that we must have knowledge and faith, in that knowledge of Jesus Christ, because through that knowledge, it has been giving us all that pertain unto life and godliness (how to live righteously). Again, we show you the importance of God, Knowledge of Jesus Christ and faith in that knowledge has given us great and mighty promises. Wherefore, enabling us to take part of his divine nature, and this heavenly nature produces within us self-control, the ability to wait with peace, living and walking in an honorable way, the ability to show friendship and love towards the

Saints and walking in agape (God-like) love. II Peter 1:8- "For if these things be in you, and abound, they make you that ye shall neither be barren nor unfruitful in the knowledge of our Lord Jesus Christ."

As a father comforting words to a child that has love and faith in their father, his words causes a child to see any situation just as the father declared it to be. In I Corinthians 15:57- "But thanks be to God, which giveth us the victory through our Lord Jesus Christ."

Also, I John 5:4- "For whatsoever is born of God overcometh the world: and this is the victory that overcometh the world, even our faith." So, hush little baby, don't you ever cry! You see, daddy has given us the victory and don't let anything cause you to deny. My child is an overcomer, that all may see, because of this, I have defeated the world and all that's within and because of my faith, I will not sin!

QUESTIONS

1. If someone ask you, "What are the steps in producing a faith that overcomes the world?" give me one or two steps that you would tell them.

2. What are characteristics or habits? Tell me in your own words.

3. In our lesson, it states that the invisible things have clearly been seen. What is it referring to?

4. In the end of our lesson, we are told that there are certain characteristics that one would do in following the word. What are these characteristics?

CHAPTER 8

Regaining Your Innocence

SESSION 1

SHUT THAT DOOR!

As we start our new study, I must first ask you to go with me on a short journey. You will need to grasp a state of being a child, and fully equip your imagination.

Let's go back into a time when there was no sin. Please note that sin is the root and offspring of all that is evil. A time when there was no sorrow, pride, schisms, divisions. A time where the word of God ruled, directed and motivated man's life and purpose for being.

Please understand that during this time, there were no sicknesses, diseases, and would you believe that there were not any deaths? Can you see it? Can you imagine it? A time of such innocence (not guilty of a crime or offence)! Man was also naked (of something such as feeling or behavior, undisguised, blatant) and free from all shame, according to Genesis 2:25- "And they were both naked, the man and his wife, and were not ashamed" (A painful feeling of humiliation or distress caused by the consciousness of wrong or foolish behavior).

Stop using your imaginations and began to realize that this time of innocence really did exist. One may ask, Please, tell me what happened? What caused events to change so drastically?

To give you the full depths of our study, we will strive to make it clear to you, the cause of certain events that put us in such a tragic condition or life situation.

A. Event #1 – Man began to value the words of Satan greater than the said word of God. Take time to consider this statement, because the reoccurrence of this event continues to cause the destruction and demise of man's very existence over and over again. A vicious and unchangeable cycle. At this time, man lost eternal life, then death took hold to mankind. Satan became man's god. John 8:43-44- "Why do ye not understand my speech? Even because ye cannot hear my word. Ye are of your father the devil, And the lusts of your father ye will do. He was a murderer from the Beginning and abode not in the truth, because there is no truth in him. When he speaketh a lie, he speaketh of his own: for he is the father of it."

B. Event #2 – Genesis 3:5-7- "For God doth know that in the day ye eat thereof, then your eyes shall be opened, and ye shall be as gods. And when the woman saw that the tree was good for food, and that it was pleasant to the eyes, and a tree to be desired to make one wise, she took of the fruit thereof, and did eat, and gave also unto her husband with her; and he did eat. And the eyes of them both were opened, and they knew that they were naked; and they sewed fig leaves together, and made themselves aprons."

We know that Adam and Eve had no sense or concept of what they were releasing among themselves and mankind, by eating of the tree that is called good and evil.

God's true desire, was for man to walk in the light of the word and live a Joyous and peaceful life. The scriptures states that their eyes were opened, Meaning that all sort of doors that were shut, had now become opened. Man's innocence was utterly gone. He began to see things in ways that God never desired for man to enter into. Man now had insight into what fear, shame, humiliation, selfishness, self-centeredness, and hatred was. In other words, man began to love the world and walk in the lust of the flesh, the lust of the eyes and the pride of life. This is why so many people that are in the world are so miserable, seeking for any way of escape, rather it be physically, mentally, chemically or even suicidal, and this all occurred because doors were opened that should have remained shut.

It is sad to say, that in the church world, there are saints that are miserable, yet while they are declaring that they are fully save and full of the holy ghost. You may ask, "Why is this?" and I will say, "because there are doors that should be closed, but yet they are still opened secretly."

I would like to give examples of some doors that causes saints secret pain and separation from God, that has truly given us the solutions to all said separations: According to Galatians 5:17-21v.- "For the flesh lusteth against the Spirit, and the Spirit against the flesh: and these are contrary the one to the other: so that ye cannot do the things that ye would. But if ye be led of the Spirit, ye are not under the law. Now the works of the flesh are manifest, which are these; Adultery, fornication, uncleanness, lasciviousness, Idolatry, witchcraft, hatred, variance, emulations, wrath, strife, seditions, heresies, Envyings, murders, drunkenness, revellings, and such like: of the which I tell you before, as I have also told you in time past, that they which do such things shall not inherit the kingdom of God." Also, unforgiveness, pains, sorrows hypocrisy, bitterness and one not totally surrendering over to Christ, whom is our total solution of getting us back from whence we have fallen.

In order for man to be able to shut the doors that were opened, he would need to die and payment made for the sins that were committed. It was impossible and still is now, for man to have the ability to pay what he owes, shut doors that should not have been opened and make the payment for sin, which is death.

According to Matthew 1:21 - "And she shall bring forth a son, and thou shalt call his name JESUS: for he shall save his people from their sins." Jesus came to save us from our sins. In other words, God almighty came to get man back from whence he had fallen. In Romans 6:3 – "Know ye not, that so many of us as were baptized into Jesus Christ were baptized into his death?" The scripture tells how Christ died, was buried and includes us as one who has died from our old man, Christ shutting all doors and paying the price that we owed including us, rewarding us with a new life and letting us know that old things has passed away, and behold, all things are become new.

Jesus Christ has showed us that, for doors to be closed, lifestyles, sinful actions, depressing thoughts and evil ways, one would have to completely die out of themself, which means that one cannot associate with it, talk about it, meditate on it, nor give into any promptings or leadings in said directions.

Metamorphous takes suffering (the state of undergoing pain, distress or hardship) through what Christ has done for me, and accepting his complete redemption of my life. I'm willing to go through whatever sufferings that are needed to break Satan's hold upon my flesh, understanding Romans 6:16- "know ye not, that to whom ye yield yourselves servants to obey, his servants ye are to whom ye obey; whether of sin unto death, or of obedience unto righteousness" that I am whatsoever I yield my member to. Passed hurts, doors of sin that I may have opened, broad paths that I have taken can all be conquered by my willingness, according to Romans 6:17-18 "But God be thanked, that ye were the servants of sin, but ye have obeyed from the heart that form of doctrine which was delivered you. Being then made free from sin, ye became the servants of righteousness."

The enemy would love for us to waste our time opening doors, causing us to be servants to envy, strife, dissimulation, division and any other works that would cause the church to be at a standstill, but we are encouraged to yield our members servants to righteousness unto holiness. Therefore, our lesson is teaching us that open doors are seeds that continue to cause problems in our lives.

Jesus Christ has truly dealt with all issues that would hinder us from getting back from our falling state. If we find ourselves not growing or developing spiritually, it is because we're not willing to suffer in the flesh to close doors that Christ has already closed and we may have reopened.

QUESTIONS

1. What did Eve do to cause doors to come open and eyes to see what eyes once did not see?

2. What is the meaning of being innocent?

3. When the lesson talks about open doors, in your words, what does this mean?

4. Why should we be willing to suffer and what will it produce?

SESSION 2

WHO HATH BELIEVED OUR REPORT?

We must start this study by showing you a glimpse of the grievous suffering of our Lord Jesus Christ.

1. He was falsely accused, tried by wicked judges, lied on by false witnesses and sentenced unjustly to a painful death.

2. During the trial, he was spit upon, opened hand slapped, brutally beaten and carried back and forth from Caiphas to Pontius Pilate, to Herod then back to Pontius Pilate. There were witnesses there that brought false accusations against Jesus.

3. The phony trial designed only to silence him and to end his ministry. You know, it is such a grievous thing when you are lied on and falsely accused by people you love and have ministered to.

4. Our Saviour was sent to Pontius Pilate, where Pilate would have freed him, but because of the bitterness of the Jews, he decided against it. Pilate brought to the front of a law that freed prisoners and exonerated him of all wrong. Jesus and Barabbas were brought before the people so that they can decide who would be set free. The people decided on that they wanted Barabbas to be freed and Jesus, crucified

5. The sentence of death was for Jesus to be whipped, then taken to a certain place and be crucified.

6. The process of Jesus being whipped, was on this wise. He was tied to what they called in that time, a whipping post that would completely reveal his entire back, where a whip that has bits of bone matter on the ends of it would slash painfully, brutally and wickedly upon his back, snatching bits of flesh each time.

7. The crucifixion was on this wise. Our Lord and Saviour, Jesus Christ was made to carry a heavy, rugged, brutal cross across his own shoulder after he was just beaten, to a place called Golgotha, where he was stretched out, arms extended, nailed separately (one at a time) upon the cross. His feet were overlapped and nailed together upon the cross. As you can see, the pain, agony and utter despair was made for payment to redeem mankind back from his fallen state.

According to I Peter 2:23-24- "Who, when he was reviled, reviled not again; when he suffered, he threatened not; but committed himself to him that judgeth righteously: Who his own self bare our sins in his own body on the tree, that we, being dead to sins, should live unto righteousness: by whose stripes ye were healed."

As we can see, what Christ paid to crucify flesh so that it would become obedient to the word of God, paying whatever necessary to accomplish one's purpose.

Take a minute to remember the Garden of Gethsemane and how the Lord fought with the flesh until he came to the conclusion that "nevertheless, is this not the purpose that I came into the world?"

Jesus Christ truly paid the price and it is complete, but if this redemption is not received, we must do whatsoever necessary (suffering) to submit ourselves to the place where the word of God is priority in our lives.

Let's take a quick journey through part of fifty-third Isaiah. The question is asked, who hath believe our report?" (give a spoken or written account of something that one has observed, heard, done or investigated). Therefore, certain facts will be presented to you as the reader, by one that had an eyewitness view of the events that occurred.

According to the report, there was nothing special or anything that would grab one's attention when it comes to the outward appearance of Christ. As a matter of fact, he was despised (contempt or a deep distaste for) and also rejected (dismissed as inadequate). In other words, he didn't fit into man's concept of the way man thought things should be.

The reporter tells us that Jesus was acquainted with sorrows (A feeling of deep distress caused by loss, disappointment, or other misfortune suffered by oneself or others) and also grief (deep sorrow, especially that caused by someone's death). The reporter also declared that we would not acknowledge him and walked away from him as though he did not exist.

Please listen to what I have seen, you, who are filled with grief. Christ has paid for that! You should be free, and your heart should be at ease, look clearly! Life would try to make you miss it! The Lord and him alone has carried our sorrows. This is where I believe that things sometimes get confusing, when we as saints, feel that we have to fix or pay for our transgressions and our iniquities. We can clearly see that by this report, the Lord Jesus has paid the price for our sins, peace and also our healing.

As one may see, all that is needed has been prepared, but as unwise sheep, mankind has strayed and the responsibility to get man back to God, has been placed on Christ.

In this lesson, we have learned the depths and the price of what was paid for our complete salvation or to get man back one with Christ. Please understand that we are part spirit, which is Christ but, also part flesh, which can result in separating us from Christ.

This is what one would need to do: Philippians 3:7-9 - "But what things were gain to me, those I counted loss for Christ. Yea doubtless, and I count all things but loss for the excellency of the knowledge of Christ Jesus my Lord: for whom I have suffered the loss of all things, and do count them but dung, that I may win Christ, And be found in him, not having mine own righteousness, which is of the law, but that which is through the faith of Christ, the righteousness which is of God by faith:"

We must be able to detach our earthly dependency or our love for material things and began to attach ourselves to Christ and the things of Christ making him priority.

Remember, that in Session one, we were showing you the importance of doors being closed and how it was so very important that we have also died with Christ. Now here we will show you the importance of the resurrection and having fellowship with the resurrection of Christ.

In Philippians 3:10-11 "That I may know him, and the power of his resurrection, and the fellowship of his sufferings, being made conformable unto his death; If by any means I might attain unto the resurrection of the dead."

It is very hard to truly know someone, until you have suffered in the same manner as they have suffered. Therefore, Paul is willing to do whatever is necessary to become more and more like Christ. In other words, Paul is saying that I am willing to die out of the flesh, that I might walk freely in the spirit.

Our lesson is striving to get us to embrace suffering with a purpose. As a caterpillar come to its end, the butterfly starts a new beginning. Paul declared in Philippians the third chapter, I don't declare that I have apprehended (understood or perceived) or even have latched onto, but I am determined and am in pursuance of becoming more in the image of the word that declares to be like Christ.

Philippians 3:12-14- "Not as though I had already attained, either were already perfect: but I follow after, if that I may apprehend that for which also I am apprehended of

Christ Jesus. Brethren, I count not myself to have apprehended: but this one thing I do, forgetting those things which are behind, and reaching forth unto those things which are before, I press toward the mark for the prize of the high calling of God in Christ Jesus."

I must remind you again. If we are to grow and develop, we are encouraged to forget those things which are behind, keeping doors shut or shutting the doors that need to be shut, not allowing anything to hinder our spiritual development.

QUESTIONS

1. Who were the three different leaders that Jesus was brought before?

2. The scripture states that Jesus learned obedience through the things he suffered. What would be one of the main things that you feel we should have learned through our suffering?

3. Give me three things that the reporter points out in his report.

4. In the end of our lesson, the scripture states that we are pressing towards a mark, in your own words, what mark are we pressing towards?

SESSION 3

IF WE SUFFER: WE SHALL ALSO REIGN WITH HIM

II Timothy 2:11-12- "It is a faithful saying: for if we be dead with him, we shall also live with him: If we suffer, we shall also reign with him: if we deny him, he also will deny us:"

There's no question, Jesus Christ reigns. In the garden of Gethsemane, the flesh and the desires of the flesh, desired Christ to disobey the will of God, which would have caused him a spiritual death.

As the battle between the flesh and the spirit took place within the mind of Christ, these words sprung forth (The Lord acknowledging the power of the father, able to do the impossible, said what we must all say, if we look to reign.) "Nevertheless not what I will" (It doesn't matter no more what I want), "but what thou wilt" (whatever you say, that is what I'm going to do).

What it means for us to reign, is that we must hear, understand and submit whole-heartily to the word of God and shut every door that leadeth to the words of Satan or our own will. This is death to the flesh.

In Matthew 7:13-14, - "Enter ye in at the strait gate: for wide is the gate, and broad is the way, that leadeth to destruction, and many there be which go in thereat: Because strait is the gate, and narrow is the way, which leadeth unto life, and few there be that find it." The word says that straight is the gate. This declares that the way of God is straight as in the garden of Eden, mankind was commanded to hear Only the voice of God and God's commandment was not to eat of the tree of Good and Evil.

People of God, it's definitely going to take a love for God and his word, to stay focused on this straight path. We are told that this path is narrow and there are not many that are willing to travel it.

There's another path that is more enticing, once one's eyes are opened. Flesh has found a place of pleasure and a satisfaction of one's carnal needs. This road is broad and has many doors that will lead one to places, depths and areas that are truly unconscionable. This broad path that we are referring to, is opened instantly when one began to listen to the voice of Satan. Such depravity (a wicked or morally corrupt act), diversity of sicknesses, state of evilness, shame and bitterness, if not closed, will bring forth death.

As the scripture declares in I Corinthians 11:30- "For this cause many are weak and sickly among you, and many sleep."

As we can see, man's pursuit leads him to a life of fear, hopelessness and fleshly desires that can never be quenched. Mankind may think that he's in charge, but as one can see, so many things have taken charge of him.

All through the bible, you will see that time and time again, for God to be able to bless mankind or even be able to use him, the flesh (man's will or desire to do his own will) must be brought under subjection and the will of God must become man's main focus.

Let me give an example of a young man that was on a course or journey to become one that reigned.

(A) Joseph reigned in his father's home through the aid of his father. His father placed him above all the other brothers, but this was not God's purpose, therefore, the Lord began to take him step-by-step on a journey. Mind you, his flesh will be brought subject, his heart will be made humble and his willingness to hold and submit to the word of God, will take him to a place where he would definitely reign.

(B) He was hated by ten of his brothers, whereas they discussed ideas of killing him, casting him in a hole and later was sold into slavery.

(C) He worked as a slave and was lied on and betrayed. At this time, in the story, one might ask "is God truly with him?" or "will God's purpose be fulfilled?"

(D) Cast into prison for something he did not do. At this time, I would like to remind you that the quicker we shut doors unto ourselves, the sooner we will see God's plan unfold.

(E) Down in the prison, Joseph would meet his main connection.

(F) Pharaoh had dreams that needed to be interpreted. Joseph, being able to interpret the dream, clearly showed the solution that resolved the upcoming problems.

(G) Pharaoh in turn gave Joseph royal status, placing him in a position under himself.

The Lord has a plan to place us back into a place where we are in our Eden (a place where we reign). That which came alive in the garden, must stay dead in our lives in order for us to be blessed in this world and the world to come.

Let us note the Prodigal son, who thought for sure that if he left his father's house, that he would reign. He left home with that which made him feel powerful, making the statement "Father, give me the portion of goods that falleth to me" In other words, "Give me what I feel is mine, that I may do with it as I please".

So many young people are living in a state where they feel that they can do whatever they will with what they feel is theirs, but the Prodigal son, leaving his father's house, not realizing that where he was, was where he needed to be and all that he ever would need, he already had. Falling and winding up in the fields to feed the swine and would have fain (willing) to have filled his belly with the husks that the swine ate, came to himself and going back to the place where he never should have left, asking the father "make me" Luke 15:17-19- "And when he came to himself, he said, How many hired servants of my father's have bread enough and to spare, and I perish with hunger! I will arise and go to my father, and will say unto him, Father, I have sinned against heaven, and before thee, And am no more worthy to be called thy son: make me as one of thy hired servants." Declaring that I have realized that I can't make myself.

We can see that it will take suffering to stay under the Father's hand and It will take suffering to stay away from any influence that would lead us out from under the Father's hand.

Look here! These scriptures let us know that we are heirs and joint heirs, but to grow and develop we would need to suffer.

Romans 8:17-18- "And if children, then heirs; heirs of God, and joint-heirs with Christ; if so be that we suffer with him, that we may be also glorified together. For I reckon that the sufferings of this present time are not worthy to be compared with the glory which shall be revealed in us."

Keep in mind the picture of the caterpillar and the butterfly!

QUESTIONS

1. What type of suffering that you believe that the lesson is referring to in order for us to reign?

2. To reign is to be in control of and have power over. Please tell me what do I suppose to have power over or in control of?

3. We were taught in the lesson that a man who is in love with his _____ will never be able to rule or reign over anything.

4. The prodigal son left his father's house saying give me, but he came back saying _____.

CHAPTER 9

SPIRIT, SOUL and BODY

SESSION 1

TOPIC: FLESH/CARNALITY

Focus Verse: I Thessalonians 5:23-"And the very God of peace sanctify you wholly: and I pray God your whole spirit and soul and body be preserved blameless unto the coming of our Lord Jesus Christ."

<u>BODY</u>

In this lesson, we will strive to give a simple understanding of three (body, flesh and carnal mind) different realities that function in our lives.

Let's take the body (the physical structure of a person, including the bones, flesh and organs). I truly would like for you to understand that my body is used to function, work and to do the necessary things physically, that I must do. My body also consist of five senses. The ears used for hearing, my nose used to smell, my mouth used to taste, my hands used to touch and my eyes used for seeing. The body certainly isn't for the use to direct me, control me nor to guide me in the way that I should go.

As individuals, we have allowed the body to be our directors or guides for many years. Now, coming to Christ, this must end. Our hopes are to tear down this way of thinking. The scriptures will plainly show one the importance of turning away from our dependency or trust in the body.

In the book of Proverbs, written by one of the wisest men (King Solomon) that ever lived, states in Proverbs 5:11-13v.- "And thou mourn at the last, when thy flesh and thy body are consumed, And say, How have I hated instruction, and my heart despised reproof; And have not obeyed the voice of my teachers, nor inclined mine ear to them that instructed me!" This body will cause one to refuse the very knowledge that would deliver it from destruction. We must turn from our dependency of the body.

As studying the word of God, it was interesting to see how one of the minor prophets warned us about our dependency of the body. In the book of Micah 6:6-8v. - "Wherewith shall I come before the LORD, and bow myself before the high God? Shall I come before him with burnt offerings, with calves of a year old? Will the LORD be pleased with thousands of rams, or with ten thousands of rivers of oil? Shall I give my firstborn for my transgression, the fruit of my body for the sin of my soul? He hath shewed thee, O man, what is good; and what doth the LORD require of thee, but to do justly, and to love mercy, and to walk humbly with thy God?" This is why it is essential for us to crucify our needs to allow the body to control us. By doing this, we will never focus on that which God requires (To do justly, love mercy and walk humbly before our God).

Let's travel now to the New Testament. The book of Matthew the fifth chapter. Matthew warns us by instructing us that the body is very passionate and will desire things so strongly, that those things will control our very lives, but Matthew is telling us to separate or cut away from any and all things that would cause us to lose sight on going back with God.

The scripture states in Matthew 5:29- "And if thy right eye offend thee, pluck it out, and cast it from thee: for it is profitable for thee that one of thy members should perish, and not that thy whole body should be cast into hell."

As we continue on in our study, we hope that your eyes are becoming enlightened and that you are seeing the need to press away from the body, understanding that in the book of Genesis, man was at peace until his eyes or senses of the body was enlightened and now we are commanded not to even consider the cries of our body, according to Matthew 6:25- "Therefore I say unto you, Take no thought for your life, what ye shall eat, or what ye shall drink: nor yet for your body, what ye shall put on. Is not the life more than meat, and the body than raiment?"

Because of the body, how many hours do we waste considering the body and its needs, worrying about what am I going to do or how to do it, or what could be done? According to Romans, we are instructed not to consider our own bodies. Romans 4:19- "And being not weak in faith, he considered not his own body now dead, when he was about an hundred years old, neither yet the deadness of Sarah's womb."

Matthew has instructed us not to esteem (hold in great respect; admired) the body, but him who is able to put body and soul into hell. Matthew 10:28- "And fear not them which kill the body, but are not able to kill the soul: but rather fear him which is able to destroy both soul and body in hell." Our aim is to utterly eradicate your confidence and hope in the body and place it on God.

Let us travel now to the book of Acts, where the demonstration of the works of the Apostles were shown. Peter shows us that the body is to be instructed, commanded and told what to do, and not it telling us what to do. Peter commanded life into a lifeless body. Acts 9:40- "But Peter put them all forth, and kneeled down, and prayed; and turning him to the body said, Tabitha, arise. And she opened her eyes: and when she saw Peter, she sat up." We see that when the body is put in check, we will freely be able to fulfill what we are called to do here upon the earth.

The more we get it and the more we come to the correct understanding, we will walk in our authority and be a blessing through Christ, to all them who are around us, as Paul did in Acts 19:12- "So that from his body were brought unto the sick handkerchiefs or aprons, and the diseases departed from them, and the evil spirits went out of them."

Walking according to the desires of our body will cause us to do as the children of Israel did, walking around and around the mountain, going nowhere.

The crucifixion must take place according to Romans 6:6- "Knowing this, that our old man is crucified with him, that the body of sin might be destroyed, that henceforth we should not serve sin." Romans 6:20-23v. "For when ye were the servants of sin, ye were free from righteousness. What fruit had ye then in those things whereof ye are now ashamed? For the end of those things is death. But now being made free from sin, and become servants to God, ye have your fruit unto holiness, and the end everlasting life. For the wages of sin is death; but the gift of God is eternal life through Jesus Christ our Lord."

It is a fact that we cannot communicate to God through the body according to lesson six. God hath given us abundant grace and the gift of righteousness, therefore, Romans 8:10 admonishes us by saying, "And if Christ be in you, the body is dead because of sin; but the Spirit is life because of righteousness." Romans 8:13v.- "For if ye live after the flesh, ye shall die: but if ye through the Spirit do mortify the deeds of the body, ye shall live."

I submit unto you, as your understanding has been opened in reference to one bringing the body, its needs and desires under subjection. You should now be able to make a bold stand and statement, as Paul did in I Corinthians 6:13v.- "Meats for the belly, and the belly for meats: but God shall destroy both it and them. Now the body is not for fornication, but for the Lord; and the Lord for the body." My body belongs to God! My whole body belongs to God!

It is a blessing to know that I am no more mine own. The Lord is my master and director in whom my body is surrendered to, according to I Corinthians 6:20v.-"For ye are bought with a price: therefore glorify God in your body, and in your spirit, which are God's."

I know as a servant of Christ, that if I am to fulfill the calling upon my life, I must bring this body under subjection, according to I Corinthians 9:27v.- "But I keep under my body, and bring it into subjection: lest that by any means, when I have preached to others, I myself should be a castaway." May I submit to you, that this is why it is hard for us to grasp lesson one (understanding and knowing our calling) and lesson two (follow me and I'll make you), because it is hard for us to put our bodies under subjection.

You know, sometimes we get so caught up in what we're doing in and through our bodies, that we fail to recognize what we are doing, whether we are doing it in the spirit of love (charity), according to I Corinthians 13:13v.- "And now abideth faith, hope, charity, these three; but the greatest of these is charity."

In 1 Corinthians 15th chapter, illustrates how beautiful it is to be sown a natural body and the transformation, once given to Christ, would take place in one's life. 1 Corinthians 15:42-44v.-

"So also is the resurrection of the dead. It is sown in corruption; it is raised in incorruption." 1 Corinthians 15:43-44v..- "It is sown in dishonour; it is raised in glory: it is sown in weakness; it is raised in power: It is sown a natural body; it is raised a spiritual body. There is a natural body, and there is a spiritual body."

QUESTIONS

1. Where in the bible that it tells us when the body became totally in focus?

2. Why do you think that it is so hard to make the transition from walking in the body, according to body?

3. What does Matthew tells us to do about things that has a hold on our body, if not delt with, can send us to hell?

4. Why is it so important to bring this body under subjection?

SESSION 2

FLESH/HUMANITY

Flesh- soft substance consisting of muscle and fat that is found between the skin and bones of a human. Flesh is sensitivity, sensual, emotional part of man that causes him to be controlled by his eyes, ears, nose, mouth and touch. Flesh is not intangible, not spiritual, it's carnal. The corruptible body of man, or corrupt nature.

In our lesson, I'm hoping that you have received a true understanding of flesh and how insignificant it is in our ability to serve the Lord.

In Genesis 6:3v.- "And the LORD said, My spirit shall not always strive with man, for that he also is flesh: yet his days shall be an hundred and twenty years." As you can see, man's fleshly state was so intolerable (unable to be endured). The Lord stated that his spirit will not always strive (make great effort to achieve or obtain something) with man.

After the creator made man, he looked and perceived that all flesh was corrupt and came to the point that he stated that "the end of all flesh is come, for the earth is filled with violence through mankind." Prompting God to destroy man with the earth.

In this study, it is imperative that you learn the severity (harshness or intense) of walking in the flesh. This fleshly state of being, causes man his own destruction and demise of the world.

As we can see, the flesh is constantly active, restless, seeking and pursuing some type of fleshly satisfaction. Psalms 38:3v. - "There is no soundness in my flesh because of thine anger; neither is there any rest in my bones because of my sin." Psalms 73:26v. "My flesh and my heart faileth: but God is the strength of my heart, and my portion for ever." This states boldly that he that walketh in the flesh shall fail.

We mentioned before and it is worth mentioning again. The flesh is intolerable and hard to be delt with, but thank God for his compassion, according to Psalm 78:38-39v.- "But he, being full of compassion, forgave their iniquity, and destroyed them not: yea, many a time turned he his anger away, and did not stir up all his wrath. For he remembered that they were but flesh; a wind that passeth away, and cometh not again."

Let us travel now into the New Testament, where we will see in the book of Matthew, that the flesh cannot discern spiritual things, nor is it able to please God, according to Matthew 16:17v.-"And Jesus answered and said unto him, Blessed art thou, Simon Barjona: for flesh and blood hath not revealed it unto thee, but my Father which is in heaven."

Matthew also shows us, that a Godly child must pray continuously to be able to walk in the strength of the spirit, because one in the flesh will only be weak according to Matthew 26:41v.- "Watch and pray, that ye enter not into temptation: the spirit indeed is willing, but the flesh is weak."

I have shown you that the flesh is truly weak and you may be asking yourself "Where is our remedy? or where is our help?" Let us travel now to the book of Acts the second chapter, which states that the Lord will pour out of his spirit upon all flesh. Acts 2:17v.- "And it shall come to pass in the last days, saith God, I will pour out of my Spirit upon all flesh: and your sons and your daughters shall prophesy, and your young men shall see visions, and your old men shall dream dreams:" Praise be to God! As you can see here, the Lord poured out his spirit, giving us the power of the Holy Ghost, transcending us from flesh to spirit!

You know, it just doesn't make any sense to me, why so many people are still striving to walk under the law. It states in the book of Romans 3:20 - "Therefore by the deeds of the law there shall no flesh be justified in his sight: for by the law is the knowledge of sin." Therefore, the law shows one how weak we are in the flesh and how much we truly need God's redemption.

As we should've come to the understanding that there's nothing truly good in the flesh, according to Romans 7:18v. - "For I know that in me (that is, in my flesh,) dwelleth no good thing: for to will is present with me; but how to perform that which is good I find not." Here, the scripture shows us a dilemma, that in my flesh (that is, walking in it) I will not be able to do that which is good. Therefore, Romans 8:1, tells me not even to walk in it (the flesh), but in the spirit. Romans 8:1v- - "There is therefore now no condemnation to them which are in Christ Jesus, who walk not after the flesh, but after the Spirit."

I have been shown a clear path from the acts and deeds of the flesh by minding the things of the Spirit according to Romans 8:5v. - "For they that are after the flesh do mind the things of the flesh; but they that are after the Spirit the things of the Spirit."

There are three stiff warnings that shows us the dangers of walking in the flesh:

Warning #1 - Romans 8:8-Those that are in the flesh cannot please God. (Romans 8:8v.- "So then they that are in the flesh cannot please God.")

Warning #2- Romans 8:9-Walking in the flesh, you have not the spirit of God, and he who have not the spirit of God, is not his (God's). (Romans 8:9v.- "But ye are not in the flesh, but in the Spirit, if so be that the Spirit of God dwell in you. Now if any man have not the Spirit of Christ, he is none of his.")

Warning #3- Romans 8:13v.-The sternest warning yet! If you walk in the flesh, ye shall die. (Romans 8:13v.- "For if ye live after the flesh, ye shall die: but if ye through the Spirit do mortify the deeds of the body, ye shall live.") These warnings should motivate us to run strongly away from the flesh towards the spiritual things of God.

1 Corinthians 1:26-29v.- "For ye see your calling, brethren, how that not many wise men after the flesh, not many mighty, not many noble, are called: But God hath chosen the foolish things of the world to confound the wise; and God hath chosen the weak things of the world to confound the things which are mighty; And base things of the world, and things which are despised, hath God chosen, yea, and things which are not, to bring to nought things that are: That no flesh should glory in his presence." As one can clearly see, the Lord is looking for yielded vessels. In other words, the Lord don't want you, he wants YOU!

So many times, we have glory seekers and those that cannot function if they can't be seen. It is certain, that the Lord knows how to humble those that refuses to humble themselves. As Paul tells us, that the Spirit of God knows how to deliver such into the hand of Satan, so that their spirit may be saved at the end, according to 1 Corinthians 5:4-5v.- "In the name of our Lord Jesus Christ, when ye are gathered together, and my spirit, with the power of our Lord Jesus Christ, To deliver such an one unto Satan for the destruction of the flesh, that the spirit may be saved in the day of the Lord Jesus."

Saints, we must be on constant guard and continue to keep our flesh under subjection. Our purpose is that Christ be manifested, according to II Corinthians 4:11v.-"For we which live are always delivered unto death for Jesus' sake, that the life also of Jesus might be made manifest in our mortal flesh."

I truly want Christ to be manifested in my walk. Therefore, I have come to this conclusion according to Galatians 2:20v.-"I am crucified with Christ: nevertheless I

111

live; yet not I, but Christ liveth in me: and the life which I now live in the flesh I live by the faith of the Son of God, who loved me, and gave himself for me." My faith must stay in God and not in my flesh.

Yes, in the book of Revelation, the Lord desires we either be hot or cold, but it was stated that we were luke warm. This occurs when one does not stay consistent in the faith and walking in the Spirit. (Revelations 3:15-16v.- "I know thy works, that thou art neither cold nor hot: I would thou wert cold or hot. So then because thou art lukewarm, and neither cold nor hot, I will spue thee out of my mouth."

Paul found such in the Galileans, according to Galatians the third chapter, he asked them a stern question. Galatians 3:3v.- "Are ye so foolish? Having begun in the Spirit, are ye now made perfect by the flesh?"

Humanity (mankind)- The human race, human beings collectively

In the book of Job, the twelfth chapter and the tenth verse, it lets us know that in the hand of God is the soul of every living thing and the breath of all mankind. Job 12:10v. - "In whose hand is the soul of every living thing, and the breath of all mankind." Mankind, as we can see, is so fragile as he may not know that he's in the hand of God. I believe that if man can comprehend just how hopeless, defenseless and how much he truly needs God, he would humble himself and turn to him (God) with all of his heart.

You know, when great catastrophe happens, as in earthquakes, title waves, great fires, storms and tornados, man can see just how helpless and hopeless that he truly is. Most of them call on God at this time, with great passion.

Here is another example of how mankind is subject and captive to that which he feels he has power over, truly have power over him and will cause him to lose eternal life according to I Corinthians 6:9-10v.- "Know ye not that the unrighteous shall not inherit the kingdom of God? Be not deceived: neither fornicators, nor idolaters, nor adulterers, nor effeminate, nor abusers of themselves with mankind, Nor thieves, nor covetous, nor drunkards, nor revilers, nor extortioners shall inherit the kingdom of God."

We have heard and do know that the flesh of mankind is a mess. James describes this, as written in James 3:14-15v.- "But if ye have bitter envying and strife in your hearts, glory not, and lie not against the truth. This wisdom descendeth not from above, but is earthly, sensual, devilish." Sensual, devilish, which causes one to look at what man sees to be uncontrollable, mankind's passion for sexual pleasures. The bible declares in Hebrews 13:4v. - "Marriage is honourable in all, and the bed undefiled: but whoremongers and adulterers God will judge." Therefore, under the honorable state of marriage, this is the only place that this is permitted.

Mankind pursuing his unquenchable nature, have been driven to a place where these desires have caused affairs, diseases, broken marriages, unwanted children, hundreds of thousands of babies killed per year, lesbianism (women with women), bestiality (sex between human and animal), lover of porn (sexual explicit material), homosexuality (men with men), in which will lead to gross darkness, which in turn leads to a reprobated mind (a state where one believes that they are right, but obviously they are wrong and refuse to listen to spiritual truths.)

QUESTIONS

1. What is the definition of flesh?

2. How can one know that they are walking in the flesh and not in the spirit?

3. Why does our lesson states that the flesh is intolerable? What does intolerable means?

4. What does Matthew 26:41 tells us that we must do?

5. What is the meaning of mankind?

6. Mankind is sensual, devilish. Explain what this means.

SESSION 3

CARNAL MINDED- If you set your mind on the things of the flesh, you are carnally minded. Carnal is where we get the word *meat* from. *Carne* is the Spanish word for meat and we see that to be carnally minded is to live after our fleshly desires.

As we can see, the depths of one being carnal can cause mankind to act and conduct himself as a pact of animals. I've seen this in fights, war, prison, men and women trying to attract one another, eating, etc.

The scripture let us know that man was born carnal, and to be carnal is to be controlled by that which one may feel that he is helpless to, according to Romans 7:14v.- "For we know that the law is spiritual: but I am carnal, sold under sin." This is a scripture that shows us that we have no choice. We <u>cannot</u> and I will repeat, We <u>cannot</u> be carnally minded according to Romans 8:6-7v.- For to be carnally minded is death; but to be spiritually minded is life and peace. Because the carnal mind is enmity against God: for it is not subject to the law of God, neither indeed can be." I pray that we take heed to this stern warning and how important it is to be not carnally minded.

Let us now go quickly to the book of 1 Corinthians, where Paul lets us know, that to be carnally minded is a sure sign of immaturity, according to Corinthians 3:1-3v.- "And I brethren, could not speak unto you as unto spiritual, but as unto carnal, even as unto babes in Christ. I have fed you with milk, and not meat: for hitherto ye were not able to bear it, neither yet now are ye able. For ye are yet carnal: for whereas there is among you envying, and strife, and divisions, are ye not carnal, and Walk as men?"

As we continue on, here in the book of 1 Corinthians and a complete study of the book will show you the many problems that Apostle Paul had with the church of God, which was at Corinth. Talking about living, acting and being carnal, this church defines it completely!

In the third chapter, Paul is warning them, that to exalt one person over another is truly being carnally minded. He was teaching them that this is the way it should be represented- We are planters and waterers. We should not be emphasizing on the laborers, but on him who will add the increase. I Corinthians 3:7v.- "So then neither is he that planteth any thing, neither he that watereth; but God that giveth the increase."

This point that Paul brings out, showing us that it is important for us to be laboring in the Kingdom, because the Lord promised to give every man his own reward according to his own labor. I Corinthians 3:7-9v.- So then neither is he that planteth anything, neither he that watereth, but God that giveth the increase. Now he that planteth and he that watereth are one: and every man shall receive his own reward according to his own labour. For we are labourers together with God: ye are God's husbandry, ye are God's building."

The Lord truly wants us to realize that the carnal mind is enmity (state or feeling of being actively opposed or hostile to someone or something) against God. I felt that it was important to go back into the book of Romans to get these two scriptures to highlight the danger of the carnal mind. Romans 8:6.-7v.-"For to be carnally minded is death; but to be spiritually minded is life and peace. Because the carnal mind is enmity against God." This is what we are fasting and praying against, the carnal mind that leads to division, stubbornness, rebellion, witchcraft, sickness, etc.

This is why it is so important to remember what was said in Romans 6:4-5v.- "Therefore we are buried with him by baptism into death: that like as Christ was raised up from the dead by the glory of the Father, even so we also should walk in newness of life. For if we have been planted together in the likeness of his death, we shall be also in the likeness of his resurrection:" The scripture is encouraging us to walk as Christ did, showing us an example as he walked in the obedience of his word and not the carnality of the flesh.

If one strives not to be carnally minded, Romans the twelfth gives us certain attributes (a quality or feature regarded as a characteristic part of someone or something), that one must have:

#1. Love without dissimulation (pretense)
#2. One must abhor (regard with disgust and hatred) all that which is evil.
#3. One must live a life, cleaving to that which is good (the word of God).

NOTE: Please remember that these attributes that we are discussing must not be done sporadically (occasionally), but must be a part of our everyday lives.

#4. We as Christians, must be kindly affectionate one to another and not every other, with brotherly love.
#5. We must honor (high respect) one another, preferring one another, even over one's self.
#6. We ought to be mature individuals, not being slow in business (the Lord's business- Matthew 6:33- But seek ye first the kingdom of God, and his righteousness; and all these things shall be added unto you.)

#7. We ought to be displaying a passionate intensity. In other words, fervent in the spirit. Therefore, we ought to have some get up and go for the things of God.

#8. Remember, a carnal mind does not think as a servant, but we as disciples must always have a mind to serve the Lord.

QUESTIONS

1. What does it mean to be carnally minded?

2. Why do the scripture states, to be carnally minded is death?

3. What were some of the problems that Paul was dealing with concerning the church of Corinth?

4. Give me three attributes of one walking in the spirit and not the Carnality of one's mind.

CHAPTER 10

The Lord Must Always Be the Center of A Disciple's Life

SESSION 1

LOVE ME WITH ALL OF YOUR HEART

Heart- Emotional sentiments which deals with seeing, hearing, touching, smelling and tasting (our senses).

In this study, we will be dealing with why the heart is our connection that makes all things happen. We will see how the heart deals with one's emotions, feelings, passions and even that which motivates us.

As the children of Israel was brought forth out of Egypt, being delivered from the power of slavery and not being able to worship God freely, even as we were delivered from our own Egypt where we were slaves and did not have the mind to worship the Lord. The Lord created and molded his people different from the world, giving them his word, which was his commandments and commanded them that, *"If thou shalt hearken unto the voice of the Lord thy God, to keep his commandments and his statutes which are written in this book of the law, and if thou turn unto the Lord thy God with all thine heart, and with all thy soul."* (Deuteronomy 30:10v.)

We will be faced with many obstacles, turmoil and troubles, but by keeping our hearts in and on the word of God, we will be able to stand and withstand.

Psalms the twenty seventh chapter and the fourteenth verse, admonishes us to wait on the Lord, even though it may seem like nothing can or will not change. This waiting that we are referring to, must be from our hearts and not from our lips. *Psalms 27:14v.- "Wait on the Lord: be of good courage, and he shall strengthen thine heart: wait, I say, on the Lord."*

As we can see, our heart directs our paths and can alter our very existence. One must keep his or her heart full of the love and joy towards the Lord and his word, to be able to stand in any season of life. We are instructed, according to *Psalms 37:4v.- "Delight thyself also In the Lord; and he shall give thee the desires of thine heart."* Here, if one can get excited about his spiritual walk from his heart with God, the blessings of God is about to flow mightily in his heart.

The enemy desires that we feel that we are missing something. Our old friends might speak to us as if things are great in the world, but we are warned, according to *Proverbs 23:17v. - "Let not thine heart envy sinners: but be thou in the fear of the Lord all the day long."* This fear is telling us to reverence (having a deep respect) God.

This study is a very serious study on the heart. If you have ever been in love with a person or had a love for a place or thing, something is always striving to take that certain thing's place. In other words, if you're in love with a person, something is always trying to show a reason why that person does not deserve your heart. Proverbs shows us that we have the power to direct the way that our heart thinks, according to Proverbs 23:7v.- *"For as he thinketh in his heart, so is he:"*

I hope that you are able to see how powerful one's heart can be. Some believe that the heart is the mind or the mind is the heart, but what is essential to know is, whatsoever you think, that is what you will be. Therefore, if you're wondering all of these years, why you are the way that you are, take time to consider the things that you have been thinking. If you think that no one likes you, they don't. If you think that nothing ever will work out for you, it won't. If you think that you can't live right, you can't. If you think that you are ugly, you are. Whatsoever one thinketh, remember this principle: that is what you are. If you think that God loves you, he does. If you think that you are anointed, you are. If you think in your heart, that you are blessed, you are. If you think that you are healed, you are. If you think that you have power over all the power of the enemy, you do. Remember this fact and never be fooled. Whatsoever one thinketh in his heart, so is he.

Let us quickly move now to the New Testament, where the Lord is commanding us once again, to love him with all of our heart. *Matthew 22:37v.-"Jesus said unto him, Thou shalt love the Lord thy God with all thy heart, and with all thy soul, and with all thy mind."*

My fellow disciples, I hope that we are able to realize how we waste so much valuable time walking in the body, feelings in the flesh and thinking carnally minded. If we would focus from our heart to love God as he requires, we would not have time to dwell in places that are not spiritually profitable.

Let me show you another essential point that needs to be considered. There are different types of hearts and, in which heart we do as Joshua was told to do in the book of Joshua the first chapter, the seventh through the eighth verse. We will be successful and able to fulfill what God has called us to do as disciples. *Joshua 1:7-8v.- "Only be thou strong and very courageous, that thou mayest observe to do according to all the law, which Moses my servant commanded thee: turn not from it to the right hand onto the left, that thou mayest prosper withersoever thou goest. This book of the law shall not depart out of thy mouth; but thou shall meditate therein day and night, that thou mayest observe to do according to all that is written therein: for then thou shall make thy way prosperous, and then thou shall have good success."*

Types of hearts:

Heart #1- A heart void of understanding. (When the word is planted, birds come and eat up the seeds. In other words, Satan snatches up the word and takes it away before it can take root.)

Heart #2- A heart that is cold, full of emotions. (When the word falls, because the grounds are stone, the roots are shallow and have no depth and when tribulations come, because of the word, they cannot stand.)

Heart #3- A heart that, when the word falls, it falls among thorns. (In other words, it is competing with the cares of this life, and eventually, those cares choke out the word and causes this person to become spiritually unfruitful.)

Heart #4- This heart is considered the heart of good ground, where the word is heard and received with understanding, causing this individual to be fruitful, spiritual and growing miraculously. Some bringing a hundredfold, some sixty, some thirty, to the building up of the Kingdom of God. This is a fact as you read and understand these four different types of hearts, that if you choose the right heart, staying in and under the word continuously and undoubtably, you will be successful in the Kingdom of God.

It is no mystery that whatever is in one's heart, it will clearly be seen and known by all, according to *Proverbs 4:23v. - "Keep thy heart with all diligence; for out of it are the issues of life."* Keeping your heart, is telling us to be careful of what we meditate upon.

Please remember that according to Proverbs 18:21 that "Death and life are in the power of the tongue." This is why our conversation, being interpreted, this is the way we live, must be holy, righteous and dedicated to the cause of the Kingdom, because what's in us, will determine what and who we are, according to Matthew 12:34v. "O generation of vipers, how can ye, being evil, speak good things? for out of the abundance of the heart the mouth speaketh." Luke 6:45v.- "A good man out of the good treasure of his heart bringeth forth that which is good; and an evil man out of the evil treasure of his heart bringeth forth that which is evil: for of the abundance of the heart his mouth speaketh."

Fellow disciples, it is truly possible for us to have a united heart towards God, according to Acts 4:32v.- "And the multitude of them that believed were of one heart and of one soul: neither said any of them that ought of the thing which he possessed was his own; but they had all things common."

QUESTIONS

1. In the book of Deuteronomy, complete this verse by filling in the blanks.

   If thou shall hearken unto the voice of the LORD thy God, to keep _____ and his _____ which are written in the book of the The law, and if thou turn unto the LORD thy God with _____ _____ _____, and with _____ _____ _____

2. The Lord tells us that he will give us something if we delight our hearts in Him. What will he give us?

3. What are the 4 different hearts?

4. From the abundance of what does the mouth speaketh?

SESSION 2

LOVE THE LORD WITH ALL THY SOUL

The word theological means the study of God and the things of God.

The theological meaning of soul is defined as the part of the individual which partakes of divinity and often is considered to survive the death of the body.

The spiritual meaning of soul refers to the part of man that connects and communicates with God. Our spirit differs from our soul, because our spirit is always pointed toward and exists exclusively for God, whereas our soul can be self-centered. The joy, comfort and peace of God's presence can only be experienced through our spirit. The soul will exist and live forever.

For us to be able to love God with all of our soul, we must have a clear understanding of what our soul truly is. Our soul is our very existence. It is what gives us our reality or our sense of being, according to Genesis 2:7v. Our very existence was created by God. *Genesis 2:7v.- "And the Lord God formed man of the dust of the ground, and breathed into his nostrils the breath of life; and man became a living soul."* Yes, as one can see, if it was not for God, we would not exist.

Is it incredible or some strange thing, that the Lord would ask of us to love him with that which he has created? Therefore, seeing that our soul must be committed to following after all the laws and commandments of our creator, knowing that this is the part of us that shall exist forever.

The Lord commanded Abraham to circumcise each male that was born the eighth day and this requirement is commanded to keep one's soul right with God, as seen in *Genesis 17:14v.- "And the uncircumcised man child whose flesh of his foreskin is not circumcised, that soul shall be cut off from his people; he hath broken mv commandment."*

One might ask, "Why would God require such a painful commitment or covenant to prove that one's soul is committed?" The answer is, because it is required of us to serve him in the completeness of oneself, and that requirement details for one to fulfill whatever is necessary to keep said commitment intact.

In serving the Lord, I must never forget that Satan is after my soul. He will strive to bring certain things that are within my life to draw my soul away from my creator.

We truly cannot ever forget the example of Adam and Eve, as they were introduced to the lust of the flesh, the lust of the eyes and the pride of life, in which had drawn their soul completely away from God, which in turn, caused the separation of their soul from God and the fall of mankind. This is why Matthew the tenth chapter reminds us, in whom we ought to reverence. *(Matthew 10:28v.- "fear not them which kill the body, but are not able to kill the soul: but rather fear him which is able to destroy both soul and body in hell.")* Therefore, after such a stern warning, our loving heavenly Father is striving to get us to see the importance of placing the right value on our relationship with him.

Our heavenly Father shows his love for something that may seem so insignificant (a sparrow). We should know that our soul must stay connected to him that knows every intimate detail about our being.

Again, the Lord is appealing to the soul of man, striving to let us know who he is, according to *Matthew 11:29v.- "Take my yoke upon you, and learn of me; for I am meek and lowly in heart: and ye shall find rest unto your souls."* Our loving Father is saying, we are truly worried and concerned about relationships, homes, money and ourselves, when all that we need to do, is to give ourselves back unto him that is meek (quiet, gentle and easily imposed on; submissive) and lowly (humble) in heart.

I feel it necessary to let you know the importance of understanding how Satan will constantly bring distractions, striving to cause one to believe that true peace is in what one possesses. The Lord emphasizes in *Matthew 16:26v.- "For what is a man profited, if he shall gain the whole world, and lose his own soul? Or what shall a man give in exchange for his soul?"*

It is so essential and so apparent that one's focus stay on God, in which all that we need will come from. According to Acts, when a man reverence God (fear him). God's grace abides upon him, as said in the forty-third verse of the second chapter of Acts. *("And fear came upon every soul: and many wonders and signs were done by the apostles.")*

Yes, we're talking about keeping our soul in tuned with God. As we can see, in this study, it is important that we would stay humble, remembering that the Lord is humble, and to have a consistent, continuing walk with him, we must walk as they walked in the book of *Acts 4:32v.- "And the multitude of them that believed were of one heart and of one soul: neither said any of them that ought of the things which he possessed was his own; but they had all things common."*

I truly would like for you to realize, that the acts of the apostles are written here in the book of Acts for an example. We saw the many trials and tribulations befall them as they strived to fulfill their mandate.

It is important that we recognize our need for one another and why it is important to support and strengthen one another *(Acts 14:21-23v.- "And when they had preached the gospel to that city, and had taught many, they returned again to Lystra, and to Iconium, and Antioch, Confirming the souls of the disciples, and exhorting them to continue in the faith, and that we must through much tribulation enter into the kingdom of God. And when they had ordained them elders in every church, and had prayed with fasting, they commended them to the Lord, on whom they believed.")*

Just as it is important to pray for one another, remember that the soul is our very existence. We must be committed to doing that which is right, holy and righteous. *Romans 2:7-11v.- "To them who by patient continuance in well doing seek for glory and honour and immortality, eternal life: But unto them that are contentious, and do not the truth, but obey unrighteousness, indignation and wrath, Tribulation and anguish, upon every soul of man that doeth evil, of the Jew first, and also of the Gentile; But glory, honour, and peace, to every man that worketh good, to the Jew first, and also to the Gentile: For there is no respect of persons with God."* As we can see, the Lord truly has no respect of persons.

The pathway and the solution to the separation caused by Adam and Eve is showing us here in 1 *Corinthians 15:45-47v.- And so it is written, The first man Adam was made a living soul; the last Adam was made a quickening spirit. Howheit that was not first which is spiritual, but that which is natural; and afterward that which is spiritual. The first man is of the earth, earthy: the second man is the Lord from heaven."*

We bring back our teaching from the beginning to re-illustrate why it is essential that our souls identify with the spirit of God, which is our soul connection to eternal life, as in the book of Malachi, God never change also in the book of Hebrews, which states that he's the same yesterday, today and forever. If our connection to him is real, then we ought to be consistent in our spiritual walk with no wavering nor shadow of turning. Sin and evil doings, ought to vex our spirit, as it did Lot. We ought to hate and despise anything that the Lord hates. *II Peter 2:8-9v. - ("For that righteous man dwelling among them, in seeing and hearing, vexed his righteous soul from day to day with their unlawful deeds:") The Lord knoweth how to deliver the godly out of temptations, and to reserve the unjust unto the day of judgment to be punished:*

*Hebrews 12:1-2v.-"Wherefore seeing (*meaning to take notice*) we also are compassed about with so great a cloud of witnesses (*meaning – striving to get our attention and our focus away from God*); let us lay aside every weight and sin which doth so easily beset us (*meaning- it is so easily to fall away from that which is true. It must be a soul, heart effort to stay away from sin*), and let us run with patience the race that is set before us (*telling us, that we should not be slothful, but because of our trust in God, we can patiently and faithfully fulfill our spiritual purpose.*); Looking unto Jesus the author and finisher of our faith; who for the joy that was set before him endured the cross, despising the shame, and is set down at the right hand of the throne of God."*

As we come to the conclusion of this lesson, I must ask these questions, "How dedicated is your soul towards the kingdom of God? Are you willing to pay what price that it would take to be transformed into a spiritual walk with God, changing one from carnal action unto spiritual actions? Are you willing to allow a hope for your soul or even willing to die for the cause of the word of God, taking full course of your life as was stated in Revelations 6:9? (*"And when he had opened the fifth seal, I saw under the altar the souls of them that were slain for the word of God, and for the testimony which they held:"*)

QUESTIONS

1. (a) What is the theological meaning of soul?

   (b) What is the spiritual meaning of soul?

2. Why is the lesson encouraging us to reverence or to fear God?

3. In the book of Acts 14:21-23v., Explain how these verses encourages us to work strongly together.

4. What state of being do a person have to be in, to be willing to die for the word of God? In other words, can anything cause you to change from your stand on the word?

SESSION 3

"AS HE IS, SO ARE WE IN THIS WORLD"

By now, you should clearly be able to see why we had to destroy all confidence in one's self, hopefully causing us to move from self-centeredness to totally being centered on Christ, which is the word. The lesson will hopefully prove to you that as Christ is, so are you in this present world.

Our two previous lessons enlightened us, in that, because of man's fall, doors were created and opened, that should have never been discovered. We were commanded thoroughly to shut these unwanted doors and to believe the report which is, that the Lord have completely given us all that is needed to live holy and righteous in this present world, understanding that one must suffer out of one's self, to totally be able to reign in a fallen world. This is why we were clearly shown just how insignificant the body is, knowing that the flesh is also insignificant and the carnal mind is death to him that walks therein. Therefore, it has been proven to us, to be able to walk with the Lord, meaning the very center of ourselves. Also, it is required that we love him with all of our soul, which is our existence, our very being.

Now, we are embarking upon that which is totally unattainable, except one learns how to walk with God with a unifying heart, soul and spirit.

Here in First John, we will begin to clearly understand that this is attainable by realizing, *"He that loveth not knoweth not God; for God is love." I John 4:8v.* Therefore, this love connection will not be reached through the body, flesh and the carnality of one's mind.

Here in the nineth verse of the fourth chapter of First John, it shows us clearly how we would be able to live a righteous life through Jesus Christ, stating that, *"In this was manifested the love of God toward us, because that God sent his only begotten Son into the world, that we might live through him." I John 4:9v.* We realize that through Christ and living through him, enables us to walk in the love or agape real kind of love of Christ.

The Lord's love was proven in how he satisfied the price that we owed through the debt that Christ paid for us, giving us access to the Lord's grace for us, as the death of Christ paid that which we owed, as Christ being the propitiation that was needed to make us united with himself. Therefore, to be one with Christ and for the love of God to be perfected in our hearts, we must love one another.

The word of God declares that, for us to be able to know that we are in him, it is by the spirit in which he has given us. Earlier up in the chapter, it declares that every spirit that does not confess that Jesus is Lord, is not of God. Therefore, if one has the love of God within them, which is God's spirit, we'll always confess that Jesus is Lord. *I John 4:16v- "And we have known and believed the love that God hath to us. God is love, and he that dwelleth in love dwelleth in God, and God in him."*

This is it! I want you to see it clearly and be able to discern what these scriptures are revealing unto you. We are truly perfected by this great love and receive boldness in the day of judgment. Listen! Listen! Listen Now! As Jesus is, so are we in this world.

When one lives as a hypocrite (declaring one thing, but living another), walking and living according to the carnality of their mind, this makes one weak and fearful, in which causes them to live in torment according to 1 *John 4:18v- "There is no fear in love; but perfect love casteth out fear: because fear hath torment. He that feareth is not made perfect in love."*

There is a wondrous, spectacular, splendid life for the Christian, knowing and understanding, that as Christ is, so are we!

Let us go to 1 Corinthians, which tells us *"But as it is written, Eye hath not seen, nor ear heard, neither have entered into the heart of man, the things which God hath prepared for them that love him."* 1 Corinthians 2:9

My fellow disciples, this scripture has been put plainly into words, what it's like walking in the supernatural spirit of Jesus Christ, 1 *Corinthians 1:10v.- "But God hath revealed them unto us by his Spirit: for the Spirit searcheth all things, yea, the deep things of God."* Whereby, we are aspiring to walk consistently in the Spirit of God and not the wisdom of man. The enemy do not want us to achieve the things that the Lord has freely opened up unto us, but it is necessary to be consistent in one's walk in the spirit of God, according to 1 *Corinthians 2:12v.- "Now we have received, not the spirit of the world, but the spirit which is of God; that we might know the things that are freely given to us of God."*

Let's take a moment to run over to Philippians the second chapter, where it tells us that, *"If there be therefore any consolation in Christ, if any comfort of love, if any fellowship of the Spirit, if any bowels and mercies, Fulfil ye my joy, that ye be likeminded, having the same love, being of one accord, of one mind. Let nothing be done through strife or vainglory; but in lowliness of mind let each esteem other better that themselves. Look not every man on his own things, but every man also on the things of others. Let this mind be in you, which was also in Christ Jesus." (Philippians 2:1-5v.)* I need for you to see how these verses are showing us that if we are to walk in the Spirit of God, having the mind of God, it must be less about us and all about living and fulfilling the purpose of Jesus Christ.

Let's go back to 1 Corinthians the Second Chapter. It was important for us to show you that humility will keep one walking in the mind and Spirit of Jesus Christ. Therefore, our very conversation must be that of the Holy Ghost and not of man's wisdom, because the natural man, meaning the body, flesh and carnal mind, receiveth not the things of the Spirit of God: for they are foolishness unto him: neither can he know them, because they are spiritually discerned.

Remember our subject, As He Is, So Are We In This World, as you read 1 *Corinthians 2:16v.- "For who hath known the mind of the Lord, that he may instruct him? But we have the mind of Christ."* This is it! This is where we want to be, understanding as it is stated in the book of *Colossians 1:27v- "To whom God would make known what is the riches of the glory of this mystery among the Gentiles; which is Christ in you, the hope of glory."* Yes! I can and will be able to achieve and accomplish great things with Jesus Christ within me.

I declare and know that I have this excellent Spirit of God, working mightily within me, enabling me to do those things that are impossible for a natural man to achieve, according to *II Corinthians 4:7v.- "But we have this treasure in earthen vessels, that the excellency of the power may be of God, and not of us."*

QUESTIONS

1. What does the word propitiation mean and why is it important to know what it means?

2. Why do love make one bold and confident, in the day of judgement?

3. What verse in our lesson is declared to show us what is the supernatural?

4. What book, chapter and verse talks about the hope of glory, and which verse talks about the excellency of the power of God?

CHAPTER 11

We Are In The Last Scene:
The Curtain of this Life is About to Close

SESSION 1

AS BEING A DISCIPLE OF JESUS CHRIST, I MUST KNOW, COMPREHEND AND HAVE THE WISDOM TO REALIZE WHAT TIME IT IS.

During the time of Noah, the Lord declared that the "*wickedness of man was great in the earth, and that every imagination of the thoughts of his heart was only evil continually. And it repented the Lord that he had made man on the earth, and it grieved him at his heart.*" (*Genesis 6:5-6v.*) In the sixth chapter of Genesis, the Lord is giving you knowledge at the extent of what was going on at that time.

Let's go on as we give you more insight, allowing you to comprehend why the Lord came to such a conclusion. The Lord said, "I will destroy man whom I have created from the face of the earth." Genesis 6:12-13v. "And God looked upon the earth, and, behold, it was corrupt; for all flesh had corrupted his way upon the earth. *And God said unto Noah, The end of all flesh is come before me; for the earth is filled with violence through them; and, behold, I will destroy them with the earth.*"

As reading the previous statements, we can clearly see why God came to such a final determination. Using your wisdom, looking, perceiving and also comparing what was going on then, to what is going on now, can you tell what time it is?

Let's go on now, to another event that God also came to a final determination on. I would like to see whether you have come to the same conclusion that the Lord came to in the book of Genesis the 18th and the 19th chapter. I believe that in the 6th chapter of the book of Genesis, that we have all come to the conclusion that the Lord destroyed all flesh, because of the evilness it derived from. We'll ask you to compare those events with what is occurring now, to see whether you believe that the events of now, warrants God coming to a determination of total annihilation (complete destruction).

The Lord came to this same determination as he looked upon the cities of Sodom and Gomorrah. These cities had fell into such a state of depravity (moral corruption; wickedness), that the cities were full of Sodomites (people who engages in anal or oral sexual intercourse).

As you perceive the knowledge of what was going on then, comprehending the severity of these events, looking and knowing what is going on now, using your wisdom, can you tell what time it is? It was important to carry you through these two events to hopefully help you to think somewhat as God does, when it comes to sin.

Let's move to the New Testament, into the book of Matthew, where we are instructed those certain events would occur when we are bordering on the end times.

In the twenty-fourth chapter of the book of Matthew, *"the disciples came unto him privately, saying, Tell us, when shall these things be? And what shall be the sign of thy coming, and of the end of the world? And Jesus answered and said unto them, Take heed that no man deceive you. For many shall come in my name, saying, I am Christ; and shall deceive many"* *(Matthew 24:3-5v.). (1 Corinthians 6:9v.- "Know ye not that the unrighteous shall not inherit the kingdom of God? Be not deceived: neither fornicators, nor idolaters, nor adulterers, nor effeminate, nor abusers of mankind"), (II Timothy 3:13v.-"But evil men and seducers shall wax worse and worse, deceiving, and being deceived."), (II John 1:7v.- "For many deceivers are entered into the world, who confess not that Jesus Christ is come in the flesh. This is a deceiver and an antichrist.")*

The Lord warns us that leaders and pastors would deceive many in the last days. Here, we will name a few that hopefully, you will realize what time it truly is.

1. Mega church Pastor, accused of allusive behavior and died of heroin and cocaine. (T.Z.)
2. Television and mega church pastor accused of immoral behavior (J. S.).
3. Mega church pastor accused of affairs with young men within the church. (E. L.)
4. Mega church pastor accused of being an antigay activist caught being gay. (T. H.)

The Lord declared also in the book of Matthew *24:6v.- "And ye shall hear of wars and rumours of wars: see that ye be not troubled: for all these things must come to pass, but the end is not yet."* The word of God is truth that can be accepted literally as it is written.

America was in a war in Iraq, which started in 2003. Now, here in year 2022, we are still fighting somewhat in Iraq. We were in war in Afghanistan for 13 years. Threats and allegations of wars coming from North Korea, China, Iran and Russia. At this very moment we are engaged in a technical war with Russia as they war against the people of Ukraine. So, we ask that you use your spiritual wisdom and divine comprehension and tell me, if you can, what time it is? *Matthew 24:7-8v.- "For nation shall rise against nation, and kingdom against kingdom: and there shall be famines, and pestilences, and earthquakes, in divers places. All these are the beginning of sorrows."* Even as you read this, these things are occurring right now.

We're coming back to the twenty-fourth chapter of Matthew, but for a moment, I would like to move to 1 Peter, to give you a clear insight of what is taking place in the church world today. The scripture states, according to 1 *Peter 4:16v. - "Yet if any man suffer as a Christian, let him not be ashamed: but let him glorify God on this behalf."* At this time, in our walk, we should have matured to a level where we are not moved by the emotions of the flesh, but are walking strongly in the spirit, according to 1 *Peter 4:17v.- "For the time is come that judgement must begin at the house of God: and if it first begin at us, what shall the end be of them that obey not the gospel of God?"*

Please note, that the angels in heaven were tested before Adam and Eve. I brought these two verses in, to introduce the next few verses in the twenty-fourth chapter of the book of Matthew. I believe that this is a spiritual furnace that will determine who is truly standing or who is just talking about standing.

Matthew 24:9-13v.- "Then shall they deliver you up to be afflicted, and shall kill you: and ye shall be hated of all nations for my name's sake. And then shall many be offended, and shall betray one another, and shall hate one another. And many false prophets shall rise, and shall deceive many. And because iniquity shall abound, the love of many shall wax cold. But he that shall endure unto the end, the same shall be saved." Here the scripture warns us of these pending events. Naturally so, around the world, in places such as China, North Korea, Tyran, Turkey, parts of Africa and Cuba.

If we look clearly, we can see these things occurring in the church world. People will murder you in the eyes of others and will destroy any credibility that you may have had with them.

The bible lets us know that where envying and strife is, there's every evil work. We are also warned against false prophets, wicked and evil leaders which will lead the people by teaching them a diluted gospel, which in turn causes them to live unholy lives. Therefore, we are instructed to hold to the truth, being faithful and committed, which will then in turn produce eternal life.

In this lesson, I've given you three different events that depicts the judgement of God being made. You were given these to hopefully help you to consider which particular time is happening now. The scripture tells us in the twenty-fourth chapter of the book of Matthew, because of who we are, we should clearly be aware of what time it truly is.

Matthew 16:2-3v.- "He answered and said unto them. When it is evening, ye say, it will be fair weather: for the sky is red. And in the morning, it will be foul weather to day: for the sky is red and lowring. O ye hypocrites, ye can discern the face of the sky; but can ye not discern the signs of the times?"

QUESTIONS

1. Why did Noah find grace in the eyes of God?

2. What was going on in Sodom and Gomorrah, to cause God to want to destroy both cities?

3. What question did the disciples ask Jesus in the twenty-fourth chapter of Matthew?

4. Different things at the end of our lesson was told to us, that we must do to have eternal life. What were they?

SESSION 2

REDEEM THE TIME

In our previous lesson, we strived to get you all to come to the conclusion that we are awaiting the coming of our Savior and Lord Jesus Christ. We all must be on one accord and know that our departure is at hand. There are certain things that we should be doing, if we believe this.

A. **Redeeming the time**-Compensating for someone's or something's faults; compensatory; able to save people from sin, error, or evil. (God's redeeming grace). In other words, makeup for lost time, pick up the pace, get in a hurry, things that should have been done; get those things done, get a consistency about one's self, knowing that there's a goal to be reached and the time is short and I must put all that I have, into reaching this goal. My life depends on it.

1. In the book of Ephesians, we are instructed boldly to redeem the time. In other words, GET IN A HURRY! The time is short! The same as the Lord told Lot, when he was instructed to leave the city, because sudden Destruction was a hand.

    The Lord is instructing us to take notice to the evil and wickedness which is around us, saying to us, as disciples, *"Wherefore be ye not unwise, but understanding what the will of the Lord is" (Ephesians 5:17)*. His will is that none should perish, nor live a riotous or wicked life, but that we walk in the spirit, according to *Romans 8:1v.- "There is therefore now no condemnation to them which are in Christ Jesus, who walk not after the flesh, but after the Spirit."*

    As disciples, we must strive to live with a joyous and pleasant Disposition. Ephesians instructs us in these words: *"Speaking to yourselves in psalms and hymns and spiritual songs, singing and making melody in your heart to the Lord; 20v.- Giving thanks always for all things unto God and the Father in the name of our Lord Jesus Christ;" (Ephesians 5:19-20)*

2. <u>Redeeming the time</u> -- Compensating (One has lost time and I must make up for lost time). Our motivation is to clearly see and to go back with the Lord. Colossians states *3:4v. - "When Christ, who is our life, shall appear, then shall ye also appear with him in glory."* Therefore, it is imperative that we kill, destroy and mortify our members which are upon the earth; fornication

(sexual intercourse between people not married to each other), Inordinate affection (anything outside of or instead of God, that you are willing to suffer for), evil concupiscence (strong desire to do evil or violate God's will), covetousness, which is Idolatry (the worship of someone or something other than God, as though it were God).

Fellow disciples, we wanted to give you these things that the scripture is telling us to mortify, and their meanings too, desiring that you would see the importance of living your life to save yourselves and to motivate others to desire to be saved. Colossians admonishes us to, *"Walk in wisdom toward them that are without, redeeming the time." (Colossians 4:5)*

B. **Keep your hope alive**- Our hope is to go back with the Lord, to **see** God. Our hope is to be transformed and to be like God. Our hope can be a strong, strong motivator, causing us to reframe, forgive, submit, overlook, press forward, deny and love, because of our hope in seeing Christ.

1 John tells us, *"Behold, what manner of love the Father hath bestowed upon us, that we should be called the sons of God: therefore the world knoweth us not, because it knew him not." (I John 3:1)*

1. (a) We are beloved of God
   (b) We are sons of God
   (c) They hated Christ, they also hate us, but we have a personal Relationship with him.

   Answer me! That hope that bums within you, isn't it yearning to one day be with Christ? Remember, that **hope** is a motivator.

Listen now, to what the second verse says- *"Beloved, now are we the sons of God, and it doth not yet appear what we shall be: but we know that, when he shall appear, we shall be like him; for we shall see him as he is." (I John 3:2)* Here in the second verse, the Lord intensifies our hope, by letting us know that we shall one day be like him.

Here, in the third verse, we are instructed to focus on verses one and two, and the belief in these verses will purify us. 1 *John 3:3v.- "And every man that hath this hope in him purifieth himself, even as he is pure."*

Now that we see the importance of redeeming the time, it is also vitally important To keep your hope alive.

The scripture warns us in the book of II Timothy the third chapter, that the times will become perilous (full of danger or risk), *"For men shall be lovers of their own selves* (A person caught up in themself, full of pride and self-centered), *covetous* (loving anything more than God), *boasters* (to praise oneself extravagantly in speech), *proud* (High regard of oneself), *blasphemers* (to speak irreverently of God or sacred things), *disobedient* (refusing to obey rules or someone in authority) to parents, *unthankful* (not showing gratitude), *unholy* (sinful; wicked), *without natural affection* (when people their instinctive love for their own parents and children), *trucebreakers* (those who violates a covenant), *false accusers* (statements that are unproven or untrue; spirit of deceit), *incontinent* (lacking self-restraint; uncontrolled), *fierce* (displaying an intense or ferocious aggressiveness), *despisers of those that are good* (utterly carnal minded and at enmity with God), *traitors* (one who betrays a friend), *heady* (intoxicating), *high minded* (arrogant; haughty), *lovers of pleasures more than lovers of God; 5v.- Having a form of godliness, but denying the power thereof: from such turn away."* We are warned here, to pull away or stay away from people who conduct themselves in such a manner. We also should realize that our lives should not represent any of these characters, if we are desiring to go back with the Lord.

QUESTIONS

1. What is the meaning of redeeming the time?

2. Why is hope so essential as we come to the end of our journey hereon earth?

3. Give me 4 things that people will be doing, during the perilous times?

4. In the book of II Peter, why are we told that, if we consider certain things, it will cause us to live a life that will be accepted before God?

SESSION 3

LEFT BEHIND

For the time is come that judgement must begin at the house of God. I do want you to realize that the scripture depicts us as being the house of God according to 1 *Corinthians 6:19v.- "What? Know ye not that your body is the temple of the Holy Ghost which is in you, which ye have of God, and ye are not your own?"* I Peter tells us, *"Ye also, as lively stones, are built up a spiritual house, an holy priesthood, to offer up spiritual sacrifices, acceptable to God by Jesus Christ." (I Peter 2:5)*

I believe that through the previous scriptures, it has been proven that we are the church, so as we study in the book of Revelation, the seven different churches, we would realize that we are referring to individuals and that it can be seven different spirits within the same church building, but if you have more individuals with the same spirit, you would have groups of people grouping together with the same spirit such as groups of Ephesus, groups of Smyrna and etc., with the self-same spirit.

The first church, which is **Ephesus**, we will see, were doing many great and wonderful things, but you will also see that they still had things that must be corrected or they will be lost. *Revelation 2:1-5v.- "Unto the angel of the church of Ephesus write; These things saith he that holdeth the seven stars in his right hand, who walketh in the midst of the seven golden candlesticks; I know thy works, and thy labour, and thy patience, and how thou canst not bear them which are evil: and thou hast tried them which say they are apostles, and are not, and hast found them liars: And hast borne, and hast patience, and for my name's sake hast laboured, and hast not fainted. Nevertheless I have somewhat against thee, because thou hast left thy first love. Remember therefore from whence thou art fallen, and repent, and do the first works; or else I will come unto thee quickly, and will remove thy candlestick out of his place, except thou repent."*

Here, as we look at **Smyrna,** the second church. Smyrna seemeth to be a strong church that stands up against those that would lie against the truth. This church will endure hard tribulations for a stand, but God hath promised that they will not hurt of the second death. Revelation 2:8-11v.- And unto the angel of the church in *Smyrna write; These things saith the first and the last, which was dead, and is alive; I know thy works, and tribulation, and poverty, (but thou art rich) and I know the blasphemy of them which say they are Jews, and are not, and are the synagogue of Satan. Fear none of those things which thou shalt suffer: behold, the devil shall cast some of you into prison, that ye may be tried; and ye shall have tribulation ten days: be thou faithful unto death, and I will give thee a crown of life.*

He that hath an ear, let him hear what the Spirit saith unto the churches; He that overcometh shall not be hurt of the second death."

The **Pergamos** church is a church that stood strongly on the word, teaching it well, not realizing that the word cuts both ways. They are warned that Satan has a seat (a stronghold in their lives) even though they are standing strong on the word. It is further said that there are among you, those that teach the teachings of Balaam and committeth fornication and these things are tolerated. Also, it was stated that the Nicolaitanes (people that ate meat that was sacrificed unto idols, also conducted elusive sexual behavior in their worships) are among you. The Lord declared that if they did not repent, his judgement will come greatly upon them, *Revelations 2:12-16v.- "And to the angel of the church in Pergamos write; These things saith he which hath the sharp sword with two edges; I know thy works, and where thou dwellest, even where Satan's seat is: and thou holdest fast my name, and hast not denied my faith, even in those days wherein Antipas was my faithful martyr, who was slain among you, where Satan dwelleth. But I have a few things against thee, because thou hast there them hold the doctrine of Balaam, who taught Balac to cast a stumbling block before the children of Israel, to eat things sacrificed unto idols, and to commit fornication. So hast thou also them that hold the doctrine of the Nicolaitanes, which thing I hate. Repent; or else I will come unto thee quickly, and will fight against them with the sword of my mouth."*

Our fourth church, is the church of **Thyatira.** As we can see, what happened in the church of Thyatira has happened in many of our churches. Allowing a spirit of whoredom and lust, to run freely throughout the church. Yes! The church did many great things and those that were standing strong were encouraged to continue to stand until the Lord's return. Please note, that the Lord knows our works and iniquity. He will judge. *Revelations 2:18-21v.- "And unto the church in Thyatira write; These things saith the Son of God, who hath his eyes like unto a flame of fire, and his feet are like fine brass; I know thy works, and charity, and service, and faith, and thy patience, and thy works; and the last to be more than the first. Notwithstanding I have a few things against thee, because thou sufferest that woman Jezebel, which calleth herself a prophetess, to teach and to seduce my servants to commit fornication, and to eat things sacrificed unto idols. And I gave her space to repent of her fornication; and she repented not."*

Let's look carefully at the grave mistakes of the church of **Sardis.** They have lost their fire, diligence and commitment to serving God. In other words, some have become weak, sick and spiritually dead and warned to recover quickly, before the Master's return. *Revelations 3:1-3v.- "And unto the angel of the church in Sardis write; These things saith he that hath the seven Spirits of God, and the seven stars; I know thy works, that thou hast a name that thou livest, and art dead. Be watchful, and strengthen the things which* *remain, that are ready to die: for I have not found thy works perfect before God. Remember therefore how thou hast received and heard, and holdfast, and repent. If therefore thou shalt not watch, I will come on thee as a thief and thou shalt not know what hour I will come upon thee."*

Unto my fellow disciples. The **Philadelphia** church exhibits the triumph spirit that we all must possess at all cost. Regardless of how hard things may seem, stand strongly to the word of God that we know. *Revelations 3:7-8v.- "And to the angel of the church in Philadelphia write; These things saith he that is holy, he that is true, he that hath the key of David, he that openeth, and no man shutteth; and shutteth, and no man openeth; I know thy works: behold, I have set before thee an open door, and no man can shut it: for thou hast a little strength, and hast kept my word, and hast not denied my name."*

The **Laodiceans** church-Well praise be to God! This is the church that I believe that hath made mammon (worldly riches; money) their God, causing them to become lukewarm in the Kingdom. Revelations 3:14-19v.- *"And unto the angel of the church of the Laodiceans write; These things saith the Amen, the faithful and true witness, the beginning of the creation of God; I know thy works, that thou art neither cold nor hot: I would thou wert cold or hot. So then because thou art lukewarm, and neither cold nor hot, I will spue thee out of my mouth. Because thou sayest, I am rich, and increased with goods, and have need of nothing; and knowest not that thou art wretched, and miserable, and poor, and blind, and naked: I counsel thee to buy of me gold tried in the fire, that thou mayest be rich; and white raiment, that thou mayest be clothed, and that the shame of thy nakedness do not appear; and anoint thine eyes with eyesalve, that thou mayest see. As many as I love, I rebuke and chasten: be zealous therefore, and repent."*

The reason, that we have taken the time to bring these churches unto you, is to show you that you might be thinking that you are doing well, and your deeds are being accepted by the Lord, but again and again, the Lord will state "Nevertheless, I have somewhat against thee." Therefore, we know what time it truly is. We need to examine, look diligently and pray sincerely unto the Lord, that he will show us anything that we need to get rid of or repent for.

Let's now go to the book of 1Thessalonians, where we are told that there's no need to emphasize the time nor the season our Lord will come. We have been taught that no man knows the time nor the hour that the Lord will come, for he shall come as a thief in the night. There will be no prior warning, other than "be ye also ready."

As man began to settle and relax, as in the times of Noah, also even now declaring that everything is peaceful and calm, trouble shall come upon mankind suddenly as a woman in travail.

Praise be to God! We are not in darkness, meaning, we are walking in the light of the word. Therefore, that day will not overtake us as those that are in darkness. *1 Thessalonians 5:5v– "Ye are all the children the children of light, and the children of the day: we are not of the night, nor of darkness."*

Surely, surely, our departure is at hand and it shall be on this wise: Those that sleep in Jesus, will God bring with him in his coming. *"For the Lord himself shall descend from heaven with a shout, with the voice of the archangel, and with the trump of God: and the dead in Christ shall rise first: Then we which are alive and remain shall be caught up together with them in the clouds, to meet the Lord in the air: so shall we ever be with the Lord." (I Thessalonians 4:16-17v.)*

Many believe that this is the rapture (rising to meet the Lord). They also believe that this is the resurrection (the event in which dead people will be brought back to life before the day of final judgement).

To get a better understanding, let's bring in 1 *Corinthians 15:51-52v.– "Behold, I shew you a mystery; We shall not all sleep, but we shall be changed, In a moment, in the twinkling of an eye, at the last trump: for the trumpet shall sound, and the dead shall be raised incorruptible, and we shall be changed."*

The scripture declares that this will happen within a moment, just as quick as one would twinkle his or her eyes. People will be taken, people will be changed. *Luke 17:34-36v. – "I tell you, in that night there shall be two men in one bed; the one shall be taken, and the other shall be left. 35v. – Two women shall be grinding together; the one shall be taken, and the other left. Two men shall be in the field; the one shall be taken, and the other left."*

The word of God is telling us that one has been taken, meaning-gone back with the Lord. The other has been left behind, which means that people that were not ready were left behind. Family members, pastors, fellow members are gone, and him that is left behind will realize the sad process of events that are about to occur. To assure that we are ready, we must do that which is righteous and stay in a state of readiness, as Paul in the book of II Timothy declared, not as one being proud, but is able to testify the state of his readiness. *II Timothy 4:6-7 v.– "For I am now ready to be offered, and the time of my departure is at hand. I have fought a good fight, I have finished my course, I have kept the faith:"*

We must know that we are ready, staying in a state of readiness and because of the times that we are in, we must know that our departure is at hand.

QUESTIONS

1. Left behind, regarding what we have just learned, what does this statement means to you?

2. Out of the 7 churches mentioned in the book of Revelations, pick 2 churches and give me their strengths and weaknesses.

3. What hope, I John 3:3v., tells us that will purify us as we are pure?

4. What is the meaning of rapture and resurrection?

5. In your own words, tell me what is the state of readiness.

CHAPTER 12

Great Sorrow As Has Never Been Seen
Upon the Earth Before/Rapture

SESSION 1

WHEN WE LEAVE AND GO TO HEAVEN

According to the book of *Isaiah 8:10v. - "For precept must he upon precept, precept upon precept; line upon line, line upon line; here a little, and there a little:"* We will be gathering together different biblical truths to show you what it will be, when we leave and go to heaven to be in the presence of Jesus.

First of all, in the book of John, the fourteenth chapter, Jesus lets us know that he will be going away and that in his Father's house, there are many mansions. *John 14:2-3v. - "In my Father's house are many mansions: if it were not so. I would have told you. I go to prepare a place for you. And if I go and prepare a place for you, I will come again, and receive you unto myself; that where I am, there ye may he also."* Now, after hearing this promise from the Lord, Thomas wanted to know, what way was the Lord referring to, and *"Jesus saith unto him, I am the way, the truth, and the life: no man cometh unto the Father, but by me." John 14:6.*

The Lord is clearly showing us that, if we abide in him and he in us, we will be ready to receive this great, magnificent promise.

Now, let's go to the book of Luke, where the Lord shows us another way that we can assure our presence in the rapture, according to Luke 24:46-49v.- *"and said unto them, Thus it is written, and thus it behoved Christ to suffer, and to rise from the dead the third day: and that repentance and remission of sins should he preached in his name among all nations, beginning at Jerusalem. And ye are witnesses of these things. And, behold, I send the promise of my Father upon you: but tarry ye in the city of Jerusalem, until ye he endued with power from on high."*

This must be our foundation, and that foundation, we must not move from.

1. We must understand the scriptures and constantly abide in them.
2. Always know and understand the suffering of Christ. In other words, having an appreciation for his suffering.
3. Know that Christ died and rose the third day. You've got to know it and <u>never</u> be shaken from that very fact.
4. We as Christians, must know that we are forgiven, save from sin and the world. Also, we must know that we are living in the spiritual, enriched, word of God and our conscious must be clear, that we are living and fulfilling these facts daily.

Let's go to the book of Acts, where Jesus was taken up into glory. I truly believe that the Lord is showing us that, to be able to rise as he did, we will need the power of the Holy Ghost.

The scripture declares that Christ was taken up from among them, and the angels proclaimed in *Acts 1:9-11v.- "And when he had spoken these things, while they beheld, he was taken up; and a cloud received him out of their sight. And while they looked steadfastly toward heaven as he went up, behold, two men stood by them in white apparel; which also said, Ye men of Galilee, why stand ye gazing up into heaven? this same Jesus, which is taken up from you into heaven, shall so come In like manner as* ye *have seen him go into heaven."*

Please note, that Jesus was caught up into heaven. John told us earlier, that Jesus went to prepare a place for us, and here, we are told that he shall return in the same manner that he had left.

Now, let us go into 1Thessalonians, which tells us how he returns and how we depart. 1 *Thessalonians 4:16-17v.-"For the Lord himself shall descend from heaven with a shout, with the voice of the archangel, and with the trump of God: and the dead in Christ shall rise first: then* we *which are alive and remain shall be caught up together with them in the clouds, to meet the Lord in the air: and so shall* we *ever be with the Lord."*

Hallelujah! Hallelujah! Hallelujah! I truly believe that this is when we will be changed, according to 1*Corinthians -"Behold, I shew you a mystery; He shall not all sleep, but* we *shall all be changed, in a moment, in the twinkling of an eye, at the last trump: for the trumpet shall sound, and the dead shall be raised incorruptible, and* we *shall be changed. For this corruptible must put on incorruption and this mortal must put on immortality. So when this corruptible shall have put on immortality, then shall he brought to pass the saving that is written, Death is swallowed up in victory."*

As we continue on precept upon precept and line upon line, keep in mind, this very fact-**So shall we ever be with the Lord!**

After the rapture, the word of God tells us that there will be a great throne. *Revelation 4:4-8v.- "And around about the throne were four and twenty seats: and upon the seats I saw four and twenty elders sitting, clothed in white raiment; and they had on their heads crowns of gold. And out of the throne proceeded lightnings and thunderings and voices: and there were seven lamps of fire burning before the throne, which are the seven Spirits of God. And before the throne there was a sea of glass like unto crystal: and in the midst of the throne, and round about the throne, were four beasts full of eyes before and behind. And the first beast was like a lion, and the second beast like a calf, and the third beast had a face as a man, and the fourth beast was like a flying eagle, And the four beasts had each of them six wings about him; and they were full of eyes within: and they rest not day and night, saying, Holy, holy, holy, Lord God Almighty, which was, and is, and is to come."*

As in our study of the scriptures, we know that the Saints will be judged and rewarded for their work, commitment and diligence towards the things of God. We believe that it was during this time, that these events occurred, because, after this, the scriptures talk about the events of the tribulation.

Listen now, to the scripture as it proclaims, *"For we must all appear before the judgment seat of Christ; that every one may receive the things done in his body, according to that he hath done, whether it be good or bad." II Corinthians 5:10v.* This judgment will not be a judgment to determine rather we go to hell or heaven, but a judgment to determine our rewards. 1 *Corinthians 3:13-15v.- "every man's work shall be made manifest: for the day shall declare it, because it shall be revealed by fire; and the fire shall try every man's work of what sort it is. If any man's work abide which he hath built thereupon, he shall receive a reward. If any man's work shall be burned, he shall suffer loss: but he himself shall be saved; yet so as by fire."* Please read the book of Matthew 25:14-46v. This will give you a clear picture of God's judgment and God's reward. Also, at this great and mighty gathering, there will be given four different and distinct crowns.

Crown 1- *The crown of rejoicing,* according to 1Thessalonians the first and second chapter. (1 Thes. 2:19v) - This crown is a crown that will be rewarded to those that win souls to the kingdom, winning souls has become a priority, and they will be rewarded greatly.

Crown 2- *The Crown of Righteousness-The* crown of righteousness will be given to those that fought a good fight, finished their course, have kept the faith and love the Lord's appearance, according to II Timothy 4:7.

Crown 3-*The Crown of Life-* This crown will be given to all those that have learned how to put the flesh under total subjection, resisting temptation, enduring steadfastly and proving their love for God, he will in turn give them a crown of life, according to James 1:12

Crown 4-*The crown of Glory-*This is a special crown, because this crown will be given to the elders that walked worthy of their calling. The Lord promised to give them the crown of Glory at his appearance, and this crown fadeth not away, according to 1 Peter 5:1-4

QUESTIONS

1. Thomas asked, how do we know the way? What was the Lord's answer?

   _____

   _____

2. What is believed to be required to meet Christ in the sky, according to Luke the 24th chapter?

3. Give me 3 things that will occur at the appearing of Jesus Christ.

4. What are the 4 crowns mentioned in our study?

* Read Revelation 7:9v.-17v. (appended to the 1st Session of the 12th Chapter)

SESSION 2

THE FIRST THREE AND A HALF
YEARS OF THE TRIBULATION

As we have learned of the occurrences that will happen after the rapture, there will also be tribulation upon the earth such as never been heard. As we can see, morality has reached an all-time low. Evil seemeth now to run rapid upon the earth. Remember the prayers of those that the word declares, availeth much, will be gone from the earth.

Matthew declares- "For then shall be great tribulation, such as was not since the beginning of the world to this time, no, nor ever shall be." (Matthew 24:21)

Let me give you some examples of the sad decay of society that will be occurring during this time. **(1) Racial Wars-** will be occurring all throughout the world, different groups will be fighting for ethnic, political, social, financial domination with such bitterness, hatred and evil that we have not seen the likes of. **(2) Political struggles-** This will cause different parties to resort to any means necessary to secure their party's success. Family/Marriages will decay to a level of moral depravity, where there will be no boundaries of what people will do or allow. **(3) Morals** will be where any type and any form of sexual pleasure that their evil minds can think of, will indulge in. **(4) The Churches** will be polluted with the acceptance of allowing any type of sin. Preaching and declaring that these things are accepted.

Let us go to the book of II Thessalonians the second chapter, where we are told, "let no man deceive you by any means: for that day shall not come, except there come a falling away first, and that man of sin be revealed, the son of perdition; Who opposeth and exalteth himself above all that is called God, or that is worshipped; so that he as God sitteth in the temple of God, shewing himself that he is God." (II Thessalonians 2:3-4v.) Also, 1 John 2:18v.- "Little children, it is the last time: and as ye have heard that antichrist shall come, even now are there many antichrists; whereby we know that it is the last time." This individual should come declaring peace and suddenly, there will be destruction upon the earth. We must consider God's people, the nation of Israel.

The events that we will now discuss, will evolve around prophecies that were prophesied concerning Israel. The word of God declares that Israel will be hated by many nations. There will be certain nations, that some believe that are directly around Israel, will rise up to eradicate them from the earth, but the Lord will fight for them, according to Ezekiel the thirty-eighth and the thirty-nineth chapter. Remember as we told you before, precept upon precept and line upon line.

Let us go now to the book of Revelation, the sixth chapter, where the seals are being opened. **Seal#1-** There was one that sitteth upon a **white horse**, with a bow and a crown which was given to him who went forth conquering and to conquer. His job is believed to conquer man and that man would be conquered by him who was on the white horse. **Seal#2-3v.-** "And when he had opened the second seal, I heard the second beast say, Come and see. 4v. And there went out another **horse** that was **red**: and power was given to him that sat thereon to take peace from the earth, (imagine earth without any peace) and that they should kill one another: and there was given unto him a great sword. **Seal#3-5v.-** And when he had opened the third seal, I heard the third beast say, Come and see. And I beheld, and lo a **black horse**; and he that sat on him had a pair of balances in his hand. 6v.-And I heard a voice in the midst of the four beasts say, A measure of wheat for a penny, and three measures of barley for a penny; and see thou hurt not the oil and the wine. **Seal#4-7v.-** And when he had opened the fourth seal, I heard the voice of the fourth beast say, Come and see. 8v.-And I looked, and behold a **pale horse**: and his name that sat on him was Death, and Hell followed with him. And power was given unto them over the fourth part of the earth, to kill with sword, and with hunger, and with death, and with the beasts of the earth. (wild animals will be attacking mankind like never before) **Seal#5-9v-**And when he had opened the fifth seal, I saw under the altar the souls of them that were slain for the word of God, and for the testimony which they held: (the promise given to those that were martyred for the Lord). **Seal#6-12v.-**And I beheld when he had opened the sixth seal, and lo, there was a great earthquake: and the sun became black as sackcloth of hair, and the moon became as blood; (earthquakes began to devastate the land, darkness was upon the earth, meteors began to hit the earth, causing nations, cities and mountains to be moved from their place. Kings, rulers and those in power, fleeing for their lives to the mountains, where they will hope for death. Revelations 6:16v.-And said to the mountains and rocks, Fallon us, and hide us from the face of him that sitteth on the throne, and from the wrath of the Lamb: 17v.- For the great day of his wrath is come; and who shall be able to stand?"

John declares that he saw four angels. Revelation 7:1-3v.- "And after these things I saw four angels standing on the four corners of the earth, holding the four winds of the earth, that the wind should not blow on the earth, nor on the sea, nor on any tree. 2v.-And I saw another angel ascending from the east, having the seal of the living God: and he cried with a loud voice to the four angels, to whom it was given to hurt the earth and the sea, 3v.-Saying, Hurt not the earth, neither the sea, nor the trees, till we have sealed the servants of our God in their foreheads."

You may be wondering, if the rapture has taken place, why are there still servants of God upon the earth? Remember, the Jews believe in God, but not in Jesus Christ, but there will be a group of Jews that will turn to God whole-heartedly.

Let us describe them, according to Revelation the seventh chapter, the fourth through the eighth verse. There will be 144,000, twelve thousand from each tribe of the children of Israel. Also, the fourteenth chapter of Revelation describes them as not being defiled with women; for they are virgins. "These are they which follow the Lamb withersoever he goeth, they were redeemed from among men, being the first fruits unto God and to the Lamb. In their mouths was found no guile and they are without fault before the throne of God," according to Revelation 14:4-5v.

I believe and many scholars, believe that these are they which will proclaim the gospel during the tribulation period. As you can see, our Savior always takes care of his own.

According to Revelations the eighth chapter, there were seven angels with seven trumpets: **Trumpet#1**- 7v.- "The first angel sounded, and there followed hail and fire mingled with blood, and they were cast upon the earth: and the third part of trees was burnt up. **Trumpet#2**-8v.-And the second angel sounded, and as it were a great mountain burning with fire was cast into the sea: and the third part of the creatures which were in the sea, and had life, died; and the third part of the ships were destroyed. **Trumpet#3**- 10v- And the third angel sounded, and there fell a great star from heaven, burning as it were a lamp, and it fell upon the third part of the rivers, and upon the fountains of waters; 11v.-And the name of the star is called Wormwood:(this is believed to be meteors falling from the stratosphere) and the third part of the waters became wormwood; and many men died of the waters, because they were made bitter. **Trumpet#4**-12v.-And the fourth angel sounded, and the third part of the sun was smitten, and the third part of the moon, and the third part of the stars; so as the third part of them was darkened, and the day shone not for a third part of it, and the night likewise. 13v.- And I beheld, and heard an angel flying through the midst of heaven, saying with a loud voice, Woe, woe, woe, to the inhabiters of the earth by reason of the other voices of the trumpet of the three angels, which are yet to sound!"

Now, entering into the nineth chapter of Revelation, **Trumpet#5**-9:1v.- "And the fifth angel sounded, and I saw a star fall from heaven unto the earth: and to him was given the key of the bottomless pit. 2v.-And he opened the bottomless pit; and there arose a smoke out of a great furnace; and the sun and the air were darkened by reason of the smoke of the pit. 3v.-And there came out of the smoke locusts upon the earth: and unto them was given power, as the scorpions of the earth have power. 4v.-And it was commanded them that they should not hurt the grass of the earth, neither any green thing, neither any tree; but only those men which have not the seal of God in their foreheads. 5v.-And to them it was given that they should not kill them, but that they should be tormented five months: and their torment of a scorpion, when he striketh a man. 6v.- And in those days shall men seek death, and shall not find it; and shall desire to die, and death shall flee from them. 7v.-And the shapes of the locusts were like unto horses prepared unto battle; and on their heads were as it were crowns like gold, and their faces were as the faces of men. 8v.-And they had hair as the hair of women, and their teeth were as the teeth of lions. 9v.-And the had breastplates, as it were breastplates of iron; and the sound of their wings was as the sound of chariots of many horses running to battle. 10v.-And they had tails like unto scorpions, and there were stings in their tails: and their power was to hurt men five months. 11 v.-And they had a king over them, which is the angel of the bottomless pit, whose name in the Hebrew tongue is Abaddon, but in the Greek tongue hath his name Apollyon. 12v.-One woe is past; and, behold, there come two woes more hereafter. **Trumpet#6**-13v.-And the sixth angel sounded, and I heard a voice from the four horns of the golden altar which is before God, 14v.-Saying to the sixth angel which had the trumpet. Loose the four angels which are bound in the great river Euphrates. 15v.- And the four angels were loosed, which were prepared for an hour, and a day, and a month, and a year, for to slay the third part of men. 16v.-And the number of the army of the horsemen were two hundred thousand thousand: and I heard the number of them. 17v. And thus I saw the horses in the vision, and them that sat on them, having breastplates of fire and of jacinth, and brimstone: and the heads of the horses were as the heads of lions; and out of their mouths issued fire and smoke and brimstone. 18v.- By these three was the third part of men killed, by the fire, and by the smoke, and by the brimstone, which issued out of their mouths. 19v.- For their power is in their mouth, and in their tails: for their tails were like unto serpents, and had heads, and with them they do hurt. 20v.-And the rest of the men which were not killed by these plagues yet Repented not of the works of their hands, that they should not worship devils, and idols of gold, and silver, and brass, and stone, and of wood: which neither can see, not hear, nor walk: 21v.-Neither repented they of their murders, nor of their sorceries, nor of their fornication, nor of their thefts."

QUESTIONS

1. Who was II Thessalonians the second chapter and the third verse talking about?

2. In our lesson, it gives us several things indicating the severity of what will be occurring with mankind. Give me two of them.

3. Please tell me, what will be going on after the angel opens the second seal?

4. Please tell me what will be occurring after the angel sounds the sixth trumpet.

SESSION 3

THE NEXT 3 AND A HALF YEARS

Now, let us continue to show the events that will be occurring during the tribulation period.

Here, in the book of Revelations the eleventh chapter, the scriptures shows us the total disregard for the Holy City and the things which are sacred. They will be trampled on for the space of forty-two months, which is three and a half years, but the Lord will raise up two witnesses that would proclaim the powers of God. They will be given great power that will astonish all the people of the existing world. If anyone hurt them, fire will proceed out of their mouths and devour their enemies. They will have power to prophesy and with that power, they will also have power to shut up heaven that it doesn't rain during their prophecy. They will also have power over the waters to turn them into blood and to smite the earth with all plagues as often as they will. These witnesses will be hated by the entire world, because they tormented them by proclaiming the word of God. Remember, to understand this great revelation, "Here a little, there a little. Precept upon precept, line upon line."

We told you that the antichrist and his false prophet were already in the world. The antichrist will grow to great power, using money, the power of military authority and great deception of craftiness, according to Daniel the eighth chapter. He will be able to deceive most of the world, even the Jewish nation. He will seem to have supernatural powers, and with these powers, he will kill the two witnesses that we talked of earlier. Their bodies will lie in the street for 3 1/2 days and the people of the world will rejoice and send gifts to one another, because of their death. "After the 3 ½ days, the spirit of life from God entered into them, they stood upon their feet and fear fell upon all of them which saw them, and they heard a great voice from heaven saying to them Come up hither! They also ascended up to heaven in a cloud and their enemies saw them."

Here, in the thirteenth chapter of John, describes these wicked and powerful men as beast. One having ten heads and one depict as a dragon. Prophesy describes these to be the antichrist and the false prophet.

1. All the world was amazed of his power and followed after him, and they worshipped the dragon (false prophet) which gave power unto the beast.
2. The scripture talks about the antichrist, but in reality, this is one that is actually proclaiming to be Christ. Many have come before him, making the same

claims, but this antichrist will come speaking great things and blasphemies, deceiving many and continue 42 months (3 ½ years), and open his mouth to blaspheme against God, to blaspheme his name, his tabernacle and them that dwell in heaven.

3. It was given unto him to make war with the Saints (those that were left behind) and to overcome them. All the nations of the world whose names are not written in the book of the Lamb will worship him.

Listen now, as the third beast appears, with two horns like a lamb, giving power to the first beast and having great power of his own.

1. He forced them which was upon the earth to worship the antichrist, which is the beast with the ten horns.
2. He has the power to make fire come down from heaven unto the earth in the **sight** of men, and deceiveth them by the means of those miracles which he had power to do in the sight of the beast.
3. The beast caused them to make an image to the antichrist which in turn gave life to the image that was created. The image that was created had power to speak and cause as many as would not worship the image of the antichrist should be killed, and he causeth all, both small and great, rich and poor, free and bond, to receive a mark in their right hand, or in their foreheads, and that no man can buy or sell, save he that had the mark or the name of the beast or the number of his name. (That number is 666). Those that has taken the mark of the beast, the seven angels were told to go their ways and pour out the vials of the wrath of God upon the earth.

Angel #1- "Poured out his vial upon the **earth,** which was a noisome and grievous sore upon them that had the mark of the beast and worshipped his image."

Angel #2- "The second angel poured out his vial upon the **sea,** and it became as the blood of dead men and every living soul died in the sea."

Angel #3- "Poured out his vial upon the **rivers and fountains of waters** and they became blood. The angels began to give glory to God saying, Lord God Almighty, true and righteous are thy judgments."

Angel #4- "poured out his vial upon the **sun** and power was given unto him to scorch men with fire and they blasphemed the name of God, which had power over these plagues; and they repented not to give him glory."

Angel #5- "poured out his vial upon the **seat of the beast** and his kingdom was full of darkness; and they gnawed their tongues for pain and blasphemed the God of heaven, because of their pains and sores and repented not of their deeds."

Angel #6- "poured out his vial upon the **great river Euphrates** and the water dried up; that the kings of the east might be prepared. The unclean spirits like frogs came out of the mouth of the dragon, and out of the mouth of the beast and out of the mouth of the false prophet. They are the spirit of the devils, working miracles, which go forth unto the kings of the earth and of the whole world, to gather them to the battle of that great day of God Almighty, which is called the battle of Armageddon."

Angel #7- "poured out his vial into the **air** and there came a voice out of the temple of heaven, from the throne saying, It is done. There were voices, thunders, lightnings and a great earth quake."

"Babylon came to remembrance before God, to give unto her the cup of the wine of fierceness of his wrath. Every island fled away and mountains were not found. Great hail out of heaven, fell upon men, every stone about the weight of a talent, and men blasphemed God because of the plague of the hail; for the plague was exceeding great."

As previously said, the Lord will destroy that wicked city Babylon, but please note that Babylon is described as a whorish woman that lie with the kings of the earth. This is describing the wicked system of filthy lucre (money gained by dishonest, or dishonorable way), promiscuous sex (having or characterized by many transient sexual relationships) and all types of deviousness. This system will be destroyed by the powers of God.

In the sixteenth chapter of the book of Revelation, it lets us know that all which is wicked, is about to come to an end through the great battle of Armageddon (the last battle between good and evil).

Now, this is the part that I am elated and highly excited to tell you about. The Lord came first, humble as a lamb, left being crucified and what seemeth like destroyed and shamefully entreated, but now, in his return, he will come arrayed in all of his glory, as the rightful King, to set all that is not in order, in order.

In the book of Jude, it tells us, "And Enoch also, the seventh from Adam, prophesied of these, saying, Behold, the Lord cometh with ten thousands of his saints, To execute judgment upon all, and to convince all that are ungodly among them of all their ungodly deeds which they have ungodly committed, and of all their hard speeches which ungodly sinners have spoken against him. These are murmurers, complainers, walking after their own lusts; and their mouth speaketh great swelling words, having men's persons in admiration because of advantage." (Jude 14-16v.)

Here, in the nineteenth chapter of the book of Revelation, it speaks of the glory of our Master and Lord and how he will be arrayed.

11v.- "And I saw heaven opened, and behold a white horse; and he that sat upon him was called Faithful and True. And in righteousness he doth judge and make war.

His eyes were as a flame of fire, and on his head were many crowns; and he had a name written, that no man knew, but he himself. And he was clothed with a vesture dipped in blood: and his name is called The Word of God. And the armies which were in heaven followed him upon white horses, clothed in fine linen, white and clean. And out of his mouth goeth a sharp sword, that with it he should smite the nations: and he shall rule them with a rod of iron: and he treadeth the winepress of fierceness and wrath of Almighty God. And he hath on his vesture and on his thigh a name written, KING OF KINGS, AND LORD OF LORDS. (Revelation 19:11-16v.)

QUESTIONS

1. The Scripture talks about two witnesses, that will come to do what? Also, what will be their power and how will they die?

2. How will the antichrist gain power and worldwide recognition and what will he do with this power and recognition?

3. What will three of the angels do, of the seven angels with the vials?

4. In the 17th and 18th chapter of the book of Revelation, it talks about a woman that is considered to be a whore, and in our lesson, we explained to you that this is a spirit. Explain to me, what type of spirit is it referring to

5. sixteenth chapter, we are introduced to the word Armageddon, what spectacular and glorious event will occur at this time and how will all this climax.

CHAPTER 13

The End of All that is and the Beginning of All That Will Be Throughout Eternity

SESSION 1

THE TWENTIETH CHAPTER OF
THE BOOK OF REVELATION

Disciples, I hope and pray that by now, you will see the importance of why it is necessary to be committed to our calling of discipleship. We see the faithfulness of the 144 thousand, their temperance (moderation or voluntary self-restraint), their dynamics of their discipline (controlled behavior) and their obedience to fulfill all that God called them to do.

As we can clearly see in the nineteenth chapter of the book of Revelation, the Battle of Armageddon did occur. It mattered less, how powerful the Antichrist and false prophet built themselves up to be, they all succumb to the power of him that rode upon the white horse, named the Word of God.

Disciples, let us go back into the twelfth chapter of the book of Revelation, that we may grasp how deceiving (cause someone to believe something that is not true, in order to gain personal advantage) and deceptive (giving an appearance or impression different from the true one; misleading) and also the spirit of pride, when Satan decided to rise above God. For this cause, Michael and his angels, fought against the dragon and his angels. *Revelation 12:7-9v.- "And there was war in heaven: Michael and his angels fought against the dragon; and the dragon fought and his angels, And prevailed not; neither was their place found any more in heaven. And the great dragon was cast out, that old serpent, called the Devil, and Satan, which deceiveth the whole world: he was cast out into the earth, and his angels were cast out with him."*

Disciples of God, the angles were in heaven and were deceived. Adam and Eve were in, Eden, which was a paradise, and they were deceived. The word of God declares in the book of II Thessalonians, that *Even him, whose coming is after the working of Satan with all power and signs and lying wonders, And with all deceivableness of unrighteousness in them that perish; because they received not the love of the truth, that they might be saved." (II Thessalonians 2:9-10v.)*

Disciples, this is a fact and needs to be repeated. The only way that we, as disciples, are going to make it, is that we love the truth with all of our heart, with all of our soul and with all our might. Jesus declared that he is the truth.

I would like to take you now, to the twentieth chapter of Revelation, where the fate (the development of events beyond a person's control regarded as determined by a supernatural power) of Satan is revealed. An angel was dispatched from heaven with orders to lay hold upon Satan and to cast him into a pit where he was to be bound a thousand years.

It is important to know that the Saints will rule the earth with Christ for this thousand-year period, as said in *Revelation 20:4v.- "And I saw thrones and they sat upon them, and judgment was given unto them: and I saw the souls of them that were beheaded for the witness of Jesus, and for the word of God, and which had not worshipped the beast, neither his image, neither had received his mark upon their foreheads, or in their hands; and they lived and reigned with Christ a thousand years."*

It is believed that the entire world will be ruled and governed by the word of God, according to the prophet Isaiah in the second chapter, which prophesied certain occurrences that shall occur.

A. The Lord shall be their judge.
B. Tools of war shall be made into tools of cultivation or farming.
C. There will be no more nation against nation and wars will be no more.
D. The lofty (proud) looks of man shall be bowed down, and the Lord alone shall be exalted in that day.
E. Idols shall be utterly abolished.
F. They shall go into the holes of the rocks, and of the earth, for fear of the Lord, and for the glory of his majesty, when he ariseth to shake terribly the earth.

Revelation 20:5-6v. - "But the rest of the dead lived not again until the thousand years were finished. Blessed and holy is he that hath part in the first resurrection: on such the second death hath no power, but they shall be priests of God and of Christ, and shall reign with him a thousand years."

I would like to interject this thought, that the Lord has promised to bless the faithful and dutiful, according to the book of *Luke 19:17v.- "And he said unto him, Well, thou good servant: because thou hast been faithful in a very little, have thou authority over ten cities."* This is where it is believed that the Lord will give certain ones rulership over certain cities.

The thousand years will come to an end. Satan will be released; his main objective will be to take over the great city that Christ established. He will compass the city with a great army that he has gathered together from all the quarters of the earth, drawing from the evil remnants that were left upon the earth. Fire came down from God out of heaven, and devoured them. *Revelation 20:10v.- "And the devil that deceived them was cast into the lake of fire and brimstone, where the beast and the false prophet are, and shall be tormented day and night for ever and ever."* Disciples of The Most High, this is the moment that we all have been looking forward to. Satan in the pit, being tormented forever. This fact had to be restated.

Now, it's time that we realize that was the last and final battle\war. Now, let us come to what will be the final judgment. *Revelation 20:11-15v.- "And I saw a great white throne, and him that sat on it, from whose face the earth and the heaven fled away; and there was found no place for them. And I saw the dead, small and great, stand before God; and the books were opened: and another book was opened, which is the book of life: and the dead were judged out of those things which were written in the books, according to their works. And the sea gave up the dead which were in it; and death and hell delivered up the dead which were in them: and they were judged every man according to their works. And death and hell were cast into the lake of fire. This is the second death. And whosoever was not found written in the book of life was cast into the lake of fire."*

QUESTIONS

1. What was the purpose of the battle that occurred in heaven?

2. Two occurrences will be going on simultaneously during the thousand-year millennial period. What will they be?

3. In the 2nd chapter of the book of Isaiah, certain events have chronologically been placed here for your information, from (A) to (F). Give me three of them in random order.

4. I thought that the battle of Armageddon was the last battle, but I see that there will be another war. Who will instigate this war and how will it end?

5. There will be a final judgment. What will this judgment be called and who will be the attendees?

SESSION 2

NEW JERUSALEM

This is a realization that must be emphasized. All of those that were not written in the Lamb's book of Life will be cast into the lake of fire. Disciples, our main focus is to help as many as we can, as well as ourselves, to ensure that all of our names be written in this book (book of life).

As we see the utter destruction and the bitter hopelessness that will fall upon mankind, this should put a spiritual motivation within our lives, causing us to fulfill our discipleship. We have learned about the heart-hardness of mankind and his total demise, seeing all that which is wicked will come to an end.

Let us now travel to the twenty-first chapter of the book of Revelation, where we will see the glorious rewards that God has prepared for his people.

The scriptures declare that there will be a new heaven and a new earth. The former heaven and earth shall pass away. John describes it, Revelation **21:2v.-** *"And I John saw the holy city, new Jerusalem, coming down from God out of heaven, prepared as a bride adorned for her husband."* (Dressed in white, pure and undefiled).

Let us describe some of the attributes of beauty that we will behold:

a. Tabernacle of God is now with men.
b. He (God) shall dwell with them and they shall be his people and he shall be with them and be their God.
c. God shall wipe away all tears from their eyes.
d. There shall be no more death, neither sorrow, nor crying, neither shall there be any more pain: for the former things are passed away.

Remember, in the scripture, the bible declares, let every word be established by two or three witnesses.

Let us now go into the book of Isaiah, that we may receive his version of this city. Isaiah stated that there will be new heavens and a new earth and the former shall not be remembered nor come into mind.

You see, Isaiah answered a question that many may have had, whether we will be concerned about those who are left behind, but it is stated that the former things will not come to mind. In Jerusalem (the city of God), God's people will ever be rejoicing!

Let us describe some of the attributes of beauty that we will behold:

a. The Lord shall rejoice within his people.
b. The voice of weeping shall not be heard anymore, nor the voice of crying, because pain, grief and sorrow will be gone forever!
c. They shall build houses, and inhabit them; and they shall plant vineyards and eat the fruit of them.
d. They shall not build and another inhabit; they shall not plant, and another eat and the elect shall enjoy the work of their hands.
e. It shall come to pass that before they call, the Lord will answer; and while they are yet speaking, he will hear.

I would like to bring to your remembrance, a promise that was given to the Philadelphia church, which is now being fulfilled in this twenty-first chapter. Revelation **3:12v.-** *"Him that overcometh will I make a pillar in the temple of my God, and he shall go no more out: and I will write upon him the name of my God, and the name of the city of my God, which is new Jerusalem, which cometh down out of heaven from my God: and I will write upon him my new name."*

The Lord commanded John to continue to write, *"I am Alpha and Omega, the beginning and the end. I will give unto him that is athirst of the fountain of the water of life freely. He that overcometh shall inherit all things; and I will be his God, and he shall be my son. But the fearful, and unbelieving, and the abominable, and murderers, and whoremongers, and sorcerers, and idolaters, and all liars, shall have their part in the lake which burneth with fire and brimstone: which is the second death." (Revelaion 21:6-8v.)* Please note, that these people have already been judged and, or casted into the lake of fire.

Now, let's get to describing our new city. John continued to describe the city as the angel called him to come and see the greatness of the city. John said, Revelations **21:10-27v.** *"And he carried me away in the spirit to a great and high mountain, and shewed me that great city, the holy Jerusalem, descending out of heaven from God, Having the glory of God: and her light was like unto a stone most precious, even like a jasper stone, clear as crystal; And had a wall great and high, and at the gates twelve angels, and names written thereon, which are the names of the twelve tribes of the children of Israel: On the east three gates; on the north three gates; on the south three gates; and on the west three gates. And the wall of the city had twelve foundations, and in them the names of the twelve apostles of the Lamb.*

And he that talked with me had a golden reed to measure the city, and the gates thereof and the wall thereof And the city lieth foursquare, and the length is as large as the breadth: and he measured the city with the reed, twelve thousand furlongs. The length and the breadth and the height of it are equal. And he measured the wall thereof, an hundred and forty and four cubits, according to the measure of a man, that is, of the angel. And the building of the wall of it was of jasper: and the city was pure gold, like unto clear glass. And the foundations of the wall of the city were garnished with all manner of precious stones. The first foundation was jasper; the second, sapphire; the third, a chalcedony; the fourth, an emerald;

The fifth, sardonyx; the sixth, sardius; the seventh, chrysolite; the eighth, beryl; the ninth, a topaz; the tenth, a chrysoprasus; the eleventh, a jacinth; the twelfth, an amethyst. And the twelve gates were twelve pearls; every several gate was of one pearl: and the street of the city was pure gold, as it were transparent glass. And I saw no temple therein: for the Lord God Almighty and the Lamb are the temple of it. And the city had no need of the sun, neither of the moon, to shine in it: for the glory of God did lighten it, and the Lamb is the light thereof And the nations of them which are saved shall walk in the light of it: and the kings of the earth do bring their glory and honour into it. And the gates of it shall not be shut at all by day: for there shall be no night there. And they shall bring the glory and honour of the nations into it. And there shall in no wise enter into it any thing that defileth, neither whatsoever worketh abomination, or maketh a lie: but they which are written in the Lamb's book of life.

QUESTIONS

1. We gave you two different comparisons of New Jerusalem. Give two ways that they are similar.

2. What way is the third chapter of Revelation compared with the twenty-first chapter of Revelation.

3. The scripture gives examples of those that did not overcome. Give me four of them.

4. New Jerusalem is described in its beauty in the twenty-first chapter. Name five views of how the glory of the city is described.

5. In the 27th verse, it tells of those that will be in this city. Who are they?

SESSION 3

RIVER OF LIFE

Here now, as we continue to depict the beauty of New Jerusalem, the sheer wonder of John's explanation of that which was revealed unto him, continues on in the twenty-second chapter of the book of Revelation.

Here John shows us, Revelation 22:1 *v.- "And he shewed me a pure river, clear as crystal, proceeding out of the throne of God and of the Lamb. As John describes this, which we as disciples have prayed, suffered, endured and pressed towards, being forever with our Lord and Savior, the Lamb of God, who has given us eternal life."*

Look now Adam, and Eve, can you see that which God had planned, which you both lost for mankind *Genesis 2:9-10v- "And out of the ground made the LORD God to grow every tree that is pleasant to the sight, and good for food: the tree of life also in the midst of the garden, and the tree of knowledge of good and evil. And a river went out of Eden to water the garden; and from thence it was parted, and became into four heads."* God has restored such, back unto us? *Revelations 22:2-3v.- "In the midst of the street of it, and on either side of the river, was there the tree of life, which bare twelve manner of fruits, and yielded her fruit every month: and the leaves of the tree were for the healing of the nations. And there shall be no more curse: but the throne of God and of the Lamb shall be in it; and his servants shall serve him."* Remember, that the curse came through yielding to the voice of Satan, which brought all the devastation, wickedness and destruction, for the past seven thousand years. Now, behold the throne of God and the Lamb, which we will be with forever! *4v.- "And they shall see his face; and his name shall be in their foreheads."* Hallelujah! Hallelujah! Hallelujah! Just to see his face! *5v.- "And there shall be no more night there; and they need no candle, neither light of the sun; for the Lord God giveth them light: and they shall reign for ever and ever."*

It is essential that I bring this following fact in, where Peter tells us, *II Peter 3:8-9v.- "But beloved, be not ignorant of this one thing, that one day is with the Lord as a thousand years, and a thousand years as one day. The Lord is not slack concerning his promise, as some men count slackness; but is long suffering to us-ward, not willing that any should perish, but that all should come to repentance."*

Listen now, to the heart of God, desiring that none be lost, but that all should come unto repentance. This is why it is essential for us as disciples to reach out with the same desire; that none be lost and that all come unto repentance.

Peter motivates the disciples to live holy, because of the wrath to come, but we also should be motivated, seeing that which will befall all unbelievers and motivated seeing the rewards that will be given to all believers.

Going back to the book of Revelation, John lets us know that these things has not occurred, but the angel revealed unto him that these things will shortly occur. John made me realize that these events are quickly approaching. Through the word of God, we realize that God's word must be obeyed and when man decides to walk in disobedience, he will fall under the wrath of God. The Lord has done for us, what I would call, the three "R's"

(a) *Redeemed* us (compensate for the faults or bad aspects of something: gain or regain possession of something in exchange for payment).

(b) *Regenerated* us (God brings a person to new life, from a previous state of separation from God and subjection to the decay of death).

(c) *Reconciliation*- He has given us the ministry of reconciliation by reconciling us unto himself and giving us the responsibility to reconcile others unto him. (God removes everything that separates man from himself, making it easy for man to come back unto him).

The purpose of this book with its thirteen lessons and thirty-nine sessions, was to prepare the disciples (student/pupil) to understand:

1. Knowing and understanding your calling (teaching one, who God called, why did God call them and what God expects from them).
2. Follow Me and I Will Make You (as one follows the leadership of Christ, he will be transformed, moving from the natural to the spiritual).
3. (A) God's Kingdom-the light, righteousness, pure holiness, (B) Satan, Darkness, Pure Evil (teaching disciples to know the differences between light and darkness, righteousness and unrighteousness).
4. Agape Love/The God Kind of Love (teaching disciples what real love is, how to walk in it and how to share it with others).
5. Indwelling Spirit of God (we were taught the power of the Holy Ghost, gift of the Spirit and benefits of walking therein).
6. We were taught on the grace of God (God giving us what we don't deserve).
7. Faith (we were taught, that without faith, it's impossible to please God, a faith that moves mountains and a faith that overcomes the world).
8. Disciples were taught how to shut doors that were once closed, and how to accept and believe that doors which were always closed; leave them closed.

9. We learned about the enemy that's in our body, flesh and the carnality of our minds.
10. Disciples realized that to be able to fulfill the calling and responsibilities that has been placed upon us, we would have to love God with all of our heart, with all our soul and to walk in the divine Spirit that was given unto us.
11. As being a disciple of Jesus Christ, I must know, comprehend and have the wisdom to realize <u>what time it is</u> (judgement is upon us).
12. Here, the disciples were taught about the rapture and the horrors of the tribulation.
13. Disciples were taught the beauty of what awaits those that have fulfilled the callings and responsibilities that God requires.

I believe that, if one is serious about the saving of themselves, their family members and of course their neighbors, that one must whole heartily grasp these teachings and apply them to their lives and share them with others, helping them in becoming true disciples of Jesus Christ.

Revelations 22:11v.- *"He that is unjust, let him be unjust still: and he which is filthy, let him be filthy still: and he that is righteous, let him be righteous still: and he that is holy, let him be holy still."*

Now, hear the words of Jesus Christ, *Revelation 22:12v.-"And, behold, I come quickly; and my reward is with me, to give every man according as his work shall be. I am Alpha and Omega, the beginning and the end, the first and the last."*

QUESTIONS

1. What did John continue to describe about the New Jerusalem in the twenty-second chapter or Revelation?

2. What are the three "R's" that we have been talking about and their significances?

3. Give me five of the thirteen lessons and what we should have learned.

4. Tell me what will happen if one embraces the lessons that have been taught?

5. What words did Jesus speak in the conclusion of this session?